CATHOLICISM AND ME

John Littleton and Eamon Maher

Catholicism and Me

the columba press

First edition, 2012, published by
the columba press
55A Spruce Avenue, Stillorgan Industrial Park,
Blackrock, County Dublin

Cover by Bill Bolger

Cover artwork, *Sacred Fragments*
(Inspired by the Franciscan church, Limerick),
by Gerry Carew

Origination by The Columba Press
Printed by MPG Books Group Ltd

ISBN 978 1 85607 864 1

Contents

Introduction

John Littleton and Eamon Maher

During the past few years, we have edited four books dealing with the challenges confronting Irish Catholicism in the third millennium.[1] Our intention in each instance was to offer readers essays that were fair and balanced, enabling them to explore Catholicism as a lived experience and facilitating them to reflect critically on the successes and failures of an institution that has moulded attitudes and opinions in Ireland for several centuries. Similar books that provide a broad cross-section of opinions on a topic that is still highly relevant are not readily available. According to certain commentators, this is due to the fact that the majority of people are no longer interested in Catholicism and are tired of reading about the failures of one of Ireland's foremost institutions to cope with the crisis that has confronted it in recent times. And yet there continues to be, in our view, a lingering, even prurient, fascination with the topic.

This is clear from the furore surrounding the May 2011 *Prime Time Investigates* television programme about Fr Kevin Reynolds (*Mission to Prey*) which revealed how some journalists, sensing the extent to which people are still fixated on the Catholic Church's legacy, will go to great lengths and take seriously irresponsible risks in order to uncover any scandal about priests and religious.[2] Investigative journalism, as exemplified by the excellent work of Mary Raftery (who died in January 2012), was to the forefront in exposing the clerical abuse scandals as well as

---

1. *Irish and Catholic? Towards an Understanding of Identity* (2006), with Louise Fuller as co-editor; *Contemporary Catholicism in Ireland: A Critical Appraisal* (2008); *What Being Catholic Means to Me* (2009); *The Dublin/ Murphy Report: A Watershed for Irish Catholicism?* (2010).

2. In the case of this television programme, sources were not checked in a proper manner before the broadcast and the reputation of an innocent man was seriously impugned. Fr Reynolds had even agreed to undergo a paternity test to prove that he had not, as was alleged, raped a woman and fathered a child by her while working as a missionary in Kenya. The national broadcaster, RTÉ, was forced to issue a full apology and pay damages as a result of this *faux pas*, which severely damaged its reputation as an impartial news agency.

corruption in financial and political circles; as such, it has performed a hugely important and necessary service to Irish society. But there can be no excuse for the type of unprofessional work that was evident in *Mission to Prey*. Too much is at stake to compromise fundamental journalistic principles.

While it is vital that the news media expose corruption and abuse wherever these may occur, there are equally occasions when the positive values associated with religion and the selfless work of priests and religious need to be emphasised, even though such topics are unlikely to make eye-catching headlines.

For example, it is rare to hear or read about the ministry of often over-worked and increasingly elderly priests in parishes throughout Ireland who visit the sick, the marginalised and the elderly, celebrate the sacraments and generally go about their work in a quiet, unobtrusive manner for salaries that would be considered derisory by others with similar qualifications working in the public or private sectors. These men are far from the 'monsters' that some people would like to depict them as being. In addition, it is appropriate to remember that CORI (the Conference of Religious of Ireland) was one of the few organisations to caution about the direction in which Ireland was headed during the heady Celtic Tiger years and the worrying gap that was developing between the rich and poor. That message frequently caused unease among those in political leadership and the business world, as CORI steadfastly championed the cause of the have-nots in society, the wounded and neglected victims of the boom times: it continues to campaign for such people today.

In an era when the negatives associated with the church as an institution are made obvious to everyone, it can be difficult for those who are committed to their Catholic identity to maintain it. Whereas, in the past, there was symbolic capital associated with being perceived to be a good Catholic, it is now almost the opposite. The status of religion in an increasingly secularised society has deteriorated to a significant degree. Charles Taylor notes in this regard:

> One understanding of secularity then is in terms of public spaces. These have been allegedly emptied of God, or any

reference to ultimate reality. Or, taken from another side, as we function within various spheres of activity – economic, political, cultural, educational, professional, recreational – the norms and principles we follow, the deliberations we engage in, generally don't refer us to God or to any religious beliefs; the considerations we act on are internal to the 'rationality' of each sphere – maximum gain within the economy, the greatest benefit to the greatest number in the political area, and so on. This is in striking contrast to earlier periods, when Christian faith laid down authoritative prescriptions, often through the mouths of the clergy, which could not be easily ignored in any of these domains, such as the ban on usury, or the obligation to enforce orthodoxy.[3]

Reflecting on Taylor's interpretation of secularity, one cannot fail to notice how succinctly it describes what happened in Ireland in recent decades. From being a model of orthodoxy, a country where the various institutions of the State were strongly influenced by Catholicism, where loyalty to Rome or deference to the dictates of bishops informed the behaviour of people in their public and private lives, we have now reached the point where religion has been relegated to a private, personal concern. This may be a positive development. We have only to recall the divisive debates and conflicting reactions to the liberal agenda in the 1970s and 1980s, when even the legalisation of the importation of contraceptives caused problems.[4]

Equally, the divorce and abortion referenda in the 1980s revealed a strong urban–rural divide and were notable for bishops' letters being read at Masses, some of which even went so far as to tell people how to vote. Yet a couple of decades later we have arrived at the point where the deference formerly shown to the church is all but obsolete. In July 2011, a landmark event

---

3. Charles Taylor, *A Secular Age* (Cambridge, Massachusetts and London: The Belknap Press of Harvard University Press, 2007), p. 2.
4. In 1973 the Supreme Court of Ireland ruled that the ban on the importation of contraceptives by married persons was unconstitutional. The following year, the legislation produced by the then Minister for Justice, Patrick Cooney, was defeated in a Dáil (Parliament) vote, with the Taoiseach (Prime Minister) of the day, Liam Cosgrave, controversially voting against his own government.

took place when An Taoiseach Enda Kenny made a scathing attack on the Catholic Church in the wake of the publication of the Cloyne Report. The fact that the comments came from the leading politician in the State who, significantly, is a practising Catholic, made their impact all the greater. In an address that contrasted starkly with the aforementioned stance adopted by a predecessor, Liam Cosgrave, Kenny made the following assertions:

- '... for the first time in Ireland, a report into child sexual abuse exposes an attempt by the Holy See to frustrate an inquiry in a sovereign, democratic republic.'
- '... the Cloyne report excavates the dysfunction, disconnection, elitism – the narcissism – that dominate the culture of the Vatican to this day. The rape and torture of children were downplayed or "managed" to uphold instead, the primacy of the institution, its power, standing and "reputation".'
- [Ireland no longer a country] 'where the swish of a soutane smothered conscience and humanity and the swing of a thurible ruled the Irish-Catholic world.'
- 'This is the "Republic" of Ireland 2011. A republic of laws, of rights and responsibilities; of proper civic order; where the delinquency and arrogance of a particular version, of a particular kind of "morality", will no longer be tolerated or ignored.'[5]

What is most significant about these comments is the way in which the speech of An Taoiseach encapsulated the *Zeitgeist* of the nation. The public reaction was generally favourable towards his presentation of the situation, which reveals a pent-up anger among Catholics and non-Catholics alike in relation to how young children suffered the most heinous crimes, sometimes perpetrated by priests about whom serious accusations had already been made, but who were allowed to continue their ministry and to have access to more hapless victims. The protestations of Cardinal Seán Brady, himself a compromised figure because of his ineffective actions as 'note-taker' for the clerical team that investigated the claims of child abuse directed at the infamous paedophile, Fr Brendan Smyth, in 1975, and other

5.   The entire speech of An Taoiseach can be accessed at http://www.rte.ie/news/2011/0720/cloyne1.html.

bishops, only serve to underline how out of touch they are with the mood of the country. While it is arguable that the allegation made by An Taoiseach about the Vatican obstructing the investigation into clerical child abuse may not have been fully justified and some of his other claims slightly exaggerated, it is indisputable that he articulated the deep feelings that have convulsed Irish people since the first trickle of revelations began to seep into the public consciousness.

In the wake of the Murphy Report, Pope Benedict XVI sent a pastoral letter to the Catholics of Ireland in which he placed the blame for clerical sex abuse predominantly on the dangerous influence of relativism and secularism:

> In recent decades, however, the Church in your country has had to confront new and serious challenges to the faith arising from the rapid transformation and secularisation of Irish society. Fast-paced social change has occurred, often adversely affecting people's traditional adherence to Catholic teaching and values. All too often, the sacramental and devotional practices that sustain faith and enable it to grow, such as frequent confession, daily prayer and annual retreats, were neglected. Significant too was the tendency during this period, also on the part of priests and religious, to adopt ways of thinking and assessing secular realities without sufficient reference to the Gospel. The programme of renewal proposed by the Second Vatican Council was sometimes misinterpreted and indeed, in the light of the profound social changes that were taking place, it was far from easy to know how best to implement it. In particular, there was a well-intentioned but misguided tendency to avoid penal approaches to canonically irregular situations. It is in this overall context that we must try to understand the disturbing problem of child sexual abuse, which has contributed in no small measure to the weakening of faith and the loss of respect for the Church and her teachings.[6]

---

6.   Text available at http://www.vatican.va/holy_father/benedict_xvi/letters/2010/documents/hf_ben-xvi_let_20100319_church-ireland_en.html. Accessed 3 August 2012.

For secularism and relativism, the Pope would have been more accurate if he had substituted clericalism and groupthink as the main reasons for the failure of the institutional church to deal with the abuse scandals. Nowhere in this response is there evidence of an acknowledgement by the Vatican that it was in any way responsible for how the bishops in Ireland reacted to the revelations about the crimes of some priests. The impression given was that clerical sex abuse was a 'local' problem, whereas it is clearly just one more example of a universal pandemic that has inflicted irreparable damage to the reputation of the institutional church. Misinterpretation by priests and religious of the documents of the Second Vatican Council (1962–5), a move away from traditional practices such as family prayer, a loss of respect for the authority of church teachings: these were some of the explanations given by the Pope for what had happened in Ireland.

Pope Benedict XVI then announced an apostolic visitation, the reports of which caused more upset among people when they became public in 2012. Once more, there is no acknowledgement of the real causes of the crisis in the Irish church in these reports. It is quite remarkable that they were published only in summary form or not made publicly available. What about transparency regarding the process that informed the findings? The recommendations included:

- The more formal segregation of seminarians from lay students in Ireland's national seminary, St Patrick's College, Maynooth. (Could this not lead to inculcating the very clerical culture that facilitated the cover-up of clerical sex abuse in the first instance?)
- Obedience to official church teaching would be demanded from priests and religious. (Several outspoken priests, for example, the Redemptorists Tony Flannery and Gerard Moloney, the Marist Seán Fagan, and the Passionist Brian D'Arcy – all of whom were judged to be theologically unsound on issues ranging from celibacy to the ordination of women, the infallibility of the Pope and the authority of the Vatican – have been censured. The public is not aware of what faults they are actually accused of, or who their detractors are.)

- The visitators attested to the great need for the Irish Catholic community to make its voice heard in the public sphere and to establish a proper relationship with the various news media, for the sake of making known the truth of the Gospel and the church's life. (But how is this consistent with the censuring of priests for publicly airing their views? Also, most Irish bishops have appeared unwilling to meet the challenge of publicly debating matters of great importance to the church such as homosexuality, the plight of the poor, married and women priests, and contraception.)

Rather than improving the situation, it seems that this intervention has merely further alienated many Irish Catholics. The American Dominican and canon lawyer, Tom Doyle, was particularly critical when assessing what the Vatican's report was attempting to do. Describing it as 'an exercise of irrelevancy', highlighted by the usual apologies, blaming the local bishops and religious superiors for not managing the situation adequately, and extolling all the church had done to eradicate the evil that was child sexual abuse, Doyle concluded: 'But in reality, they looked for excuses rather than explanations. This "crisis" is not primarily about sexual molestation. It's about the obsession with power and the corruption and stagnation of the clerical culture.' According to him, 'the total lack of accountability by the authoritarian model of the church is the root of the crisis'.[7]

Returning to the model of church as monarchy, where the centralised bureaucracy in Rome ensures adherence to orthodoxy and obedience, is this the best way to emerge from the current impasse? The cleavage between what are commonly described as the liberal and the conservative camps within the Catholic Church means that it is especially difficult for the institution to speak with one voice. Those clerics who dare to stray from the party line, those who have the courage to express their views on issues like married and women priests, for example, are now being censured. Surely it would be better to debate these matters in an open manner and convince people, lay and

---

7. Tom Doyle, 'Vatican Report attempts mere excuse not explanation', in *The Irish Times*, 27 March 2012.

clerics alike, of the validity and reasonableness of the church's teaching?

While the sexual abuse scandals have played a significant role in the decline of the Catholic Church's influence in Ireland, they are only part of a greater sentiment of religious disillusionment that began to take root as early as the 1960s. Higher disposable income, the arrival of television, increased access to education, foreign travel, the dance hall phenomenon, pop music, the women's liberation movement, have all resulted in the emergence of at least two generations of Irish people who are no longer prepared to follow automatically the church's official teaching regarding issues of individual conscience, particularly in the sexual domain. The notion of being punished or struck down by a harsh God who oversees all our actions ceased to hold sway as religious doctrines and their implications for living were subjected to rational analysis and were sometimes found to be lacking in common sense and logic. Consequently, they were ignored by many, without necessarily bringing about a break with the church, which continued to exert power and influence.

The Eucharistic Congress was held in Ireland for the first time in 80 years in 2012. Instead of the triumphalistic celebration of Ireland's unique commitment to Catholicism and the huge attendances of 1932, the 2012 version could be characterised as having been a much more low-key affair. In general, the church and state in Ireland now operate independently of each other and while a sizeable majority of the Irish population still regard themselves as being Catholic – at least nominally – attendance at Sunday Mass and the regular celebration of the sacraments have decreased significantly. In some parishes in Dublin, for example, Mass attendance is as low as 5 per cent of the Catholic population. A survey of Irish Catholics carried out by Amárach Research on behalf of the Association of Catholic Priests found that the church's teaching on sexuality had 'no relevance' for 75 per cent of respondents and their families. In addition, 87 per cent of respondents believed that priests should be allowed to marry and 77 per cent were in favour of women priests.[8]

---

8. The full findings of the survey are available at http://www.amarach. com/assets/files/ConsumerForesightArchive/ACP%20Survey%20Findi ngs%20April%202012.pdf. Accessed 3 August 2012.

However, the disconnection between official church teachings and the way in which Catholicism is lived and practised by
ordinary church members should not result in a denial of the
cultural attachment that still exists in Ireland to the majority
religion. On the eve of the 2012 Eucharistic Congress, *The Irish
Times* editorial, 'Church at a Crossroads', noted the sea-change
in attitudes that has taken place in the past 80 years: 'That world
is dead', it stated. 'Ireland will never again be a monolithic
culture in which a single hierarchal institution can enjoy such
prestige.' In order for the church to find its bearings in the new
Ireland, the editorial argued, there is a need to build bridges
between those who would favour a return to the discipline
and certainties of the past and the 'cultural Catholics' who find
church teaching on certain moral issues like contraception to be
obsolete or meaningless and yet who feel as though their identity
is strongly marked by Catholicism. The editorial concluded:

> What's so terrible about 'cultural Catholicism' – the idea
> that the broad church is deeply intertwined with the way
> Irish people think and feel and, however occasionally,
> pray? There is a deep well of respect and affection for
> Catholic tradition even among those who do not wish to
> obey an all-male celibate elite and who make up their
> own minds about spiritual and moral questions. If the
> church pushes such people away, it will make itself a
> sad and bitter thing and, in the process, impoverish Irish
> culture as a whole.[9]

While some within the church may well question the desir-
ability of cultural or *à la carte* Catholicism, it is the form of religion espoused by an ever-increasing number of people on this
island at present. Irish Catholicism will never disappear completely and although in all likelihood it will not attract the same
numbers to its ceremonies in the future or impact seriously on
the moral choices most people make, it could well find renewed
vigour among those who choose to commit wholeheartedly to
its survival.

Catholicism and Me (even if the phrase is, strictly speaking,
ungrammatical!) is an attempt to encourage further and informed debate around the fallout that has emerged in the wake

---

9.   'Church at a Crossroads', editorial in *The Irish Times*, 9 June 2012.

of the Catholic Church's serious demise in Ireland. It contains the reflections of people from various backgrounds and spiritual convictions who kindly agreed to disclose the fruits of their interaction with Roman Catholicism. The contributors include bishops, journalists, politicians, theologians, people from business and academic backgrounds, and those working in inner city Dublin and in the prison service. They share an intimate knowledge of Catholicism from inside or outside the institutional church. Some are believers, others are not sure about exactly where to position themselves. But, irrespective of categorisations or affiliations, their ponderings capture the unique role that Catholicism has played and continues to play in contemporary Ireland.

As in previous volumes, we have invited different voices to address the reader so that a fuller picture may emerge of the positive and negative experiences that Catholicism has imparted to each contributor. We thank them for their often painstaking and candid accounts and we are confident that their reflections will resonate with many people in Ireland and abroad. Thus we invite you to read what they have written so that you may appreciate for yourself what a valuable contribution they have made by communicating their relationship with a religious tradition that may well be in crisis, but is far from dead.

Engaging with Catholicism

Willie Walsh

My first reaction to the invitation to write something about my 'engagement with Catholicism' was that it hasn't been just an engagement; rather, it has been a lifelong marriage. My life is imbued with Catholicism and on reflection I am not sure where the 'me' begins or ends in terms of separating my personal identity as a human being from my religion. A lifetime of 'being a Catholic' has made less clear the boundaries that exist between personal identity, personal faith and religion. All three are synonymous for me at this point as I enjoy the autumn/winter of my life on God's earth.

I was born in 1935 and grew up in an Ireland where faith and practice was simply part of life. Few if any boundaries existed between citizenship and Catholicism, between faith and religion. Obedience to God and one's superiors was a necessary ingredient for living any kind of worthwhile life. I believe that part of my motivation to become a priest was based on a desire to save my own soul. In time this matured into a desire to help and to serve others. I have no doubt that the fear of God also figured highly in that motivation process. That too has thankfully changed over the years as my image of God became more gentle and compassionate. There was no room or thought given to what suited my personality or as to what human qualities I possessed that suited me for priesthood or were perhaps better suited to another way of life. There was a narrowness about Catholicism in my early life that excused itself on the grounds of an absolute conviction that the Catholic Church was the one and true church and therefore there could be no doubt that the best possible thing one could do with one's life was to become a priest.

In hindsight, after all the intervening years, one marvels at the astounding simplicity of one's faith as well as the unequivocal control the Catholic Church's teaching had over one's life. I went to St Patrick's College Maynooth to study for the priesthood and after three years there I was sent to the Irish College in Rome to complete my studies. I was happy in Maynooth and its strict regime caused me no concern as I was at that time a very diligent and disciplined student. I accepted Maynooth's quite rigid routine of prayer and study with no great difficulty. Indeed I was sad to leave there after three years, but I quickly adapted to the less rigid system that existed in the Irish College in Rome. I believe that the more relaxed atmosphere of the Irish College loosened that personal rigidity that had been fostered by both my upbringing and by Maynooth. I found myself far more at home with the Italian approach of *catolico ma non fanatico* than with the rule and fear-dominated Irish church of the time. This Roman interlude helped me greatly in moving towards a kinder and gentler church in line with my evolving image of God.

I was ordained in 1959 and after some further study in Rome I returned in 1962 to the Irish church that had hardly changed in the intervening years. It was a church still deeply confident in its own rightness, and indeed righteousness. Mass attendance was very high; people went to confession regularly and attended sodalities and parish missions in large numbers. It was an era of the triangular model of church with the Pope at the apex, then the bishops and next the priests. The laity was at the base of the triangle and their role was to 'pray, pay and obey'. The priest welcomed you into the world at baptism, nourished your life with the Eucharist and saw you out of this world with the sacrament of extreme unction. To die without the priest was the ultimate tragedy. Inevitably this gave a power beyond merit to priests and hierarchy and created a church that was rigid and at times somewhat oppressive.

Change was at hand, however, and the 1960s was a period of great renewal not only in the church but in all of society worldwide. Pope John XXIII convened the Second Vatican Council with great promise of renewal and change for the church in the modern world. John F. Kennedy became the first Catholic President of the United States and Harold McMillan was speaking of the 'winds of change blowing through Africa' as that continent's countries sought their independence. Seán Lemass crossed the border to meet Terence O'Neill. Changes took place in culture, in almost every facet of people's lifestyles. Civil rights were in the air. All these changes were resisted in some shape or other. Some church leaders feared that people would not be able to cope with a modernisation of the church. Yet change cannot be held back forever and so the world and the church in my lifetime accommodated the changes as best it could.

It was an exciting time to be a Catholic. I was impatient with the pace of change in the implementation of Vatican II's new outlook. I regularly met with a small group of fellow priests to help one another prepare our Sunday sermons and to discuss pastoral issues. We were all eager to see the church move forward in the spirit of Vatican II. We were viewed with some suspicion by older and wiser priests in the diocese. I was then teaching mathematics and science in St Flannan's College, Ennis, County Clare and I remember with affection the many students who were 'angry, young men', impatient to change the world. I wonder how much of my own being an angry, young priest impatient to change the church rubbed off on them or did they even notice it? I often regret the passing of 'the angry, young men'.

The changes of Vatican II took hold very gradually but despite our impatience many of us did find changes to be good when they finally took root. We welcomed changes such as the development of adult religious education, pre-marriage courses, parish councils and a new emphasis on the role of lay people in the church. There were obvious external changes such as the vernacular language of the Mass, where Latin was set aside in favour of priest and people celebrating together in a language understood by all. 50 years after Vatican II it is ironic that one of the most controversial changes to take place recently is the introduction of the new Missal which sought to alter the earlier modern language versions by replacing them with a more literal translation of the older Latin Mass.

But the 1960s were not all about change. Advances in medicine in relation to fertility control brought into question the church's position on family planning. Pope Paul VI set up a commission to examine the issue. There was a strong expectation that there might be a change in the church's teaching. In

July 1968 Pope Paul VI issued his encyclical *Humanae Vitae* which reasserted the traditional teaching on sexuality and family planning. The reaction to the encyclical was quite controversial. For many it was the only possible decision that the Pope could have given. Change to such teaching was unthinkable. For many who anticipated and hoped for change it was a deep disappointment. Not adhering to church teaching is as old as the church. But this was different. Very many theologians, some priests and even bishops either questioned the teaching or tried to interpret it in a manner that would lessen its impact. There was much debate in relation to the role of conscience. In this regard most couples of child-bearing age simply ignored it. They felt that the teaching placed an unbearable burden on their relationship.

At a personal level, 1968 was a significant year in my own priesthood. I was involved in setting up the Catholic Marriage Advisory Council (CMAC) in our diocese. For the next 42 years I worked closely with CMAC (later ACCORD) at diocesan level as priest director and later at national executive level as bishops' representative. That involvement was a most enriching experience. It was affirmative and supportive of my priesthood. It was challenging in that one worked side by side on equal terms with married people. It gave me privileged insight into marriage and sexuality which no seminary training could have given. And the people with whom I worked gave me a quality of friendship and love which I did not experience anywhere else in the church.

Life continued through the 1970s and 1980s. It was a very busy and fulfilling life with full-time teaching, involvement in ACCORD and working with marriage tribunals. That is not to say that it was all plain sailing in regard to my own priesthood. At a certain period I began to sense that the excitement and enthusiasm of the earlier years of priesthood was beginning to wane. I began to wonder if I had made the right decision in becoming a priest in the first instance. Wouldn't it be lovely to have married and to have had children? There is inevitably that sense of aloneness in the celibate priesthood that I believe is more acute during one's 40s and 50s. And then more unsettling questions arise. How can you be sure that Catholicism has got it all right? I never had any difficulty about the person of Jesus Christ or about the values he preached and held – truth and justice, forgiveness, compassion and love. But I was no longer as sure as I would like to be where faith was concerned. And when you have doubts like that should you leave the priesthood? Yet I stayed and there is no simple answer to the question: Why did I stay? I cannot say that there was a specific decision to stay. I still believed very strongly that my work both in teaching and ACCORD was very worthwhile. I believe that these and the deep friendship and love I experienced within a small number of families sustained me throughout that period of personal difficulties. And perhaps the change from teaching to parish work which happened in 1988 gave something of a renewed purpose to my priesthood. It was not as if all questions and doubts suddenly disappeared. It was rather that the daily public celebration of the Eucharist, being with people in their joys and sorrows particularly in baptisms and funerals, the celebration of marriage and visiting of the housebound gave a more natural setting to faith and priesthood.

I was appointed coadjutor Bishop of Killaloe in June 1994. I expected to have a leisurely introduction to the office but Bishop Michael Harty died suddenly in early August and I had to take on the office right away. I served as bishop for 16 years until my retirement in August 2010. Looking back from the comfort of retirement and reflecting on those 16 years spent as bishop, some things stand out for me. Overall, I was happy as a bishop and at a human level I received generous support from the priests and people of the diocese for which I will always be grateful. In hindsight, it is humbling to realise how good they were to me. Even though my life as bishop was extremely busy and pressured, I was always aware that being a bishop was both a privilege and a responsibility.

It was a privilege to lead the people of Killaloe in the living of their faith and to experience their support and their love and a responsibility to fulfil that task of leadership to the best of my ability.

I was privileged to work with my colleague priests in re-sponding to the pastoral needs of the people of the diocese which brought with it a responsibility for me as bishop to also care for the needs of these priests.

It is the privilege of a bishop to administer the sacrament of confirmation to thousands of young people across the diocese and it is his responsibility to help these young people to feel special and sacred on this occasion, in addition to touching the lives of their parents and extended families.

There was the deeply painful privilege to be allowed listen to the hurts of people, especially the terrible hurts of victims of sexual abuse, and to try insofar as possible to help towards healing. There was the grave responsibility to do all in one's power to respond appropriately to all victims of sexual abuse as well as dealing in an appropriate way with sexual offenders. I felt great personal distress over the scandal of child sexual abuse. It is a distressing matter for all in the church and it took us in church leadership a long time to face up to it. It was the single most heart-breaking issue and the most time consuming during my years as bishop. It took up more time than any other pastoral concern. I never saw it as time wasted, however, and in the light of what victims have suffered I have no doubt there was no other issue more worthy of the time I gave to it.

Throughout my time as bishop I lived with a constant tension between trying to be faithful to the teaching of the church and my own personal feelings in relation to the pastoral care of people whose lives were regarded as being in some way at variance with the teaching of said church. This in turn led to tension in my relationships with ecclesiastical authorities in Rome. When the Apostolic Nuncio informed me in June 1994 that I was to become a bishop, I made known to him that I had worries in relation to certain areas of church teaching. I mentioned in particular the areas of sexuality and family planning. I suggested to him that he might wish to look at my views again and that I had no difficulty if he then concluded that I was unsuited to be a bishop. His response was that all of us experienced doubts and that he was satisfied that I should accept the appointment.

I did not anticipate that this tension between church teaching and my own pastoral instincts would become a significant issue for me over the coming years. I gradually found myself questioning and asking for more discussion on issues such as compulsory celibacy, the exclusion of people in second unions from the sacraments, the undervaluing of the role of women in our church, our teaching on sexuality and family planning. I was regularly told firmly by the Roman authorities that my task as bishop was to teach and explain church teaching. They were clear that it was not a bishop's role to raise questions or to seek discussion on these matters.

Let me be clear that I do take very seriously my commitment to church teaching. I also respect the authorities in Rome who called me to task on these matters and do not question their sincerity and their commitment to our church. I regret and am saddened by our inability to resolve that tension between us. I am only too well aware that so many people have to live with tensions between their ideals and their lived reality. How many parents have to live with the tension between their beliefs and the way their children live? And yet they never withdraw their love for their children. While we as church may claim that we too never withdraw our love and care for people whose lives are in conflict with our own teaching, it seems to me that it must be very hard for such people to see us as a loving church. Of course when one asks for more discussion of these issues some people feel that one is being disloyal and indeed I have often asked that question to myself and wondered am I lacking in the courage to stand up for church teaching regardless of how it affects people's lives?

We have become accustomed to saying that the church in Ireland and worldwide is in crisis. Some see the crisis as rooted solely in the abuse scandals, others see it as a crisis born out of failure to be true to the orthodox teaching of the church. More see the crisis as existing in the clash between the church and a very secular-minded world. Crisis is something that always existed for the church as it attempted to preach the gospel of Christ through the centuries. Any of the aforementioned issues is a crisis and needs to be addressed and dealt with in healthy realistic ways. It will also require time, patience and respect for everyone's position in order to move through any or all of these crisis points.

I believe that the basic message of Christ's call to 'follow me' needs to be foregrounded in the lives of all Christians as we face any crisis in this life. We need to focus more and more on Christ, on his example, his teaching and his call to 'follow me'. I sense a desire from the Vatican and among a small number of younger clergy to roll back the changes which followed Vatican II. I don't believe this 'rolling back' is a solution to any crisis facing the church. I don't however dismiss those who feel the need to 'roll back'. It is a time for dialogue but it must be a dialogue in which all viewpoints are respected, where freedom of expression is accepted and where each one is free to express his or her own truth in love. I find it impossible to accept that certain topics are beyond discussion.

In August 2010 I retired as bishop and I was happy to welcome Fr Kieran O'Reilly SMA as my successor. Bishop Kieran with his missionary background brings a new and rich experience to the leadership of the diocese. I had anticipated that stepping down would be somewhat traumatic. It was not. In fact, the overwhelming feeling was a sense of personal freedom now that I had handed over the responsibility of office to someone else. While the years as bishop had been happy and quite fulfilling, I had no difficulty in letting go. I suppose at 75 one no longer has the energy to work 12/14-hour days, to have one's life regulated by the clock, to respond to so many different calls on one's time and to carry the burden of responsibility which goes with being a bishop at this time. A hurling metaphor may be apt here in that one sees things somewhat differently when one sits in the stand rather than pacing the sideline.

I find myself now more and more inclined to leave the future with the Lord. I believe the world and the church is in his hands and that he will ultimately lead us in the right path. I trust in the Lord who challenged Peter three times with the question: 'Do you Love me?' (John 21:15–17) and then spoke those unsettling words to Peter: 'I tell you most solemnly,/When you were young/you put on your own belt/and walked where you liked;/but when you grow old/you will stretch out your hands,/and somebody else will put a belt round you/and take you where you would rather not go' (John 21:18).

I like to think that in recent years the Lord has been leading us to places we would rather not have gone but we trust in him and in his love to lead us through. Our church is founded on

Christ's love and his love has room for the firm believer and the doubter, the saint and the sinner. My engagement/marriage with that church over a lifetime has been a relatively happy one but like most marriages it has had its times of significant tension and pain. If, however, I were asked to renew the marriage vows I believe I would still reply 'I do'.

The fire burns within my heart, imprisoned in my bones …

Angela Hanley

'Why do you *bother*?' I have been asked this many times by people who cannot understand my wish to remain a member of the church and to struggle for a place there. I can answer this question, but rather than a simple 'because …', the answer is the story of my life. Given that I was born in 1959, the year John XXIII called his Council, share a birthday with Karl Rahner and have Michael Curley, the formidable Archbishop of Baltimore and Washington, in my ancestry, maybe I was never going to get very far from church, despite my best efforts. I belonged to an ordinary working-class family whose day-to-day concerns were more immediate than many of those who followed the proceedings of the Council. I was raised in an environment that respected the sacred without undue deference to the clerical caste, with a common-sense approach to life. There was no excessive scrupulosity, yet boundaries between right and wrong were very clear. Though there was no undue deference to priesthood, there was always a sense of the priest being an educated man, who knew all there was to be known. The respect was for his education more than his office.

For all that, my Catholic religious rearing was mostly benign, both at home and at school. I always kept a space between God and the hierarchical church. This seems to have been instinctive and fundamental to my thinking. I was not a person who was moved by May altars, processions or Benediction. I believe the person of faith that I have become was always there. To put words on that experience is not now anachronistic. It is finally to have words to describe what was for many years inchoate. Who I am now is the logical progression of the little person I was then. I think it was always more a case of 'God and me' than 'Catholicism and me'. Yet the only way it was possible to reach this God was through Catholicism, or so it appeared from my experience. I had no other term of reference.

My earliest conscious experience of Catholicism was exclusion, or at best, acceptance on sufferance. Girls were somehow
second-best. My awakening came with the realisation that girls
could not be altar servers. Before the term 'institutional misogyny' entered my consciousness, I knew it was grossly unfair that I
could not serve simply because I was a girl. At six years of age I
felt the unfairness of this to the very marrow of my bones. I did
not feel angry about it. I did not know that I should be angry at
this. It was just the way of things. The maleness of participation
was so ingrained in the people and the fabric of Irish
Catholicism that questions simply did not arise – certainly not in
my environment. And yet, for all the questions that were never
asked, Catholicism, as I lived it, never sat wholly comfortably
with me.

As for God, again despite all the images presented of a
bearded man, God remained a presence in my life but never
clearly defined as male. I have tried to analyse this as an adult –
how could I relate to all the male imagery and the use of male
language without making God male? I still have no answer, or
rather the answer remains: God is a surrounding presence that
defies definition in human terms. God as presence was an image
that was imprinted on my soul in the formative event of my
childhood – the death of an older brother when he was 19 years
old, and I just 10. Growing with and through the unfathomable
pain of that loss helped me understand that 'God's will' is not
something we can claim to know. How could it be God's will
that such pain would come crashing through a family? This was
a further loosening of an already tenuous grip of Catholicism on
my evolving intellect. The puppet-master God, who controlled
everything on a whim, was not my God. The God whose
presence and constancy sustained me through unspeakable loss
is the God who has remained.

I had a brief association with the charismatic movement in
my mid-teens. And although I did not stay with it, it bequeathed
me a treasure – the scriptures. For that I will always be grateful.
My Bible became and has remained my *vade mecum*. My searching heart found an echo in the Wisdom literature, Psalms, Isaiah
and the Gospel of John. Again, by instinct, I knew that although
the Bible was understood to be the word of God, it was not to be

taken literally. The simplest reading shows up inconsistencies that ought to alert any attentive reader. Though much of my experience as a Catholic has been anything but inspiring, scripture always nourished my mind, my heart and my soul. I remember thinking how much I would have loved to study scripture more fully, but again – that was not open to me. There was no full theological programme available to non-clerics at the time. Again, being female was to be 'less than', to be excluded.

Catholicism as exclusion continued into my adult life. When our parish opened up the ministries of the Word and of the Eucharistic, I was wholly invisible. My husband was asked to serve three terms as both. Eventually, when they ran out of all the obvious candidates for Ministry of the Eucharist, I was worth considering. I found being a Eucharistic minister a moving experience, particularly in my own preparation for it. It meant much to me, for the short time I served. It was with more than a little sadness that I opened the parish news bulletin one day and discovered that the Mass at which I served was abolished, and my service with it. While some other ministers were bitterly disappointed and quite angry at the lack of consultation, I was altogether more sanguine. To me it was just another manifestation of the exclusion that was my continued experience of Catholicism, and another push along the road to separation. The only question was: When would the sundering take place? By now I had two teenage children and I stayed for their sakes. Once my daughter was old enough to argue her case for refusing to attend Mass or having anything to do with church, I could not with any integrity argue against her. Her older brother soon followed her lead. I could no longer see any future for myself within Catholicism.

When I was making my preparation to leave the church in the late 1990s, I happened to read *Does Morality Change?* by Seán Fagan SM. This book was the seminal event of my adult Catholicism. For the first time in my life, I felt someone was speaking to me as an intelligent, adult Catholic. It caused me to pause and rethink. Seán and I became good friends and I was blessed to have a theological mentor of his calibre just at the moment I needed it and was ready for it. I am a questioner by nature – I always needed to know the 'why' of things. As with all the best teachers, Seán never directly answered my 'whys'. He gave me the material and waited to see what I would make of it, and then affirmed my response. It was exhilarating! It was the best possible theological grounding before any formal studies began. It meant that I took no aspect of theology at face value. I realised that the phrase 'church teaching' is a very ambiguous term. Who or what is 'church'? Whose cultural milieu is setting the agenda for the 'teaching'? Who has the competence to teach? Do the teachers understand that life is an evolving process, not a series of philosophical propositions? Do the teachers themselves believe they have anything to learn? To whom do the teachers listen – if they listen at all? I bounced everything against my experience, realising that theology must speak to praxis if it is to have any value. Ivory-tower theology may be immensely satisfying intellectually, but if it does not find grounding in the reality of people's lives, it is largely irrelevant, as are its practitioners. I say this as one naturally inclined to the academic.

The intuitions of my childhood were affirmed and expanded by my experience of doing theology. God was one thing, organised religion, another – they are not synonymous. It was a revelation to see that Greek philosophy has had a far greater influence in the formation of Catholicism, as we know it, than scripture. There were many other such epiphanies in my education that all acted as a collective spiritual sigh that said 'at last ... now it all makes sense ... now the pieces fit'. However, this was not the end of the journey. This was just one more step along the way.

In my experience as an apprentice theologian, I came across many people like myself, for whom Catholicism was more about exclusion than *communio*. Also, there was a disturbing pattern whereby the more empowered people became, the more they seemed to be feared by their priests. I meet an ever-increasing number of people who identify themselves with the excluded as Catholics. This is a slow but steady movement. Owen O'Sullivan aptly named it 'the silent schism' in the title of his 1997 book, and it continues to grow. There is a marked reluctance in the church's leadership to acknowledge this exodus of Catholics as a symptom of something quite rotten at the heart of Catholicism's own administration. It is much more comfortable to label it individualism, materialism or secularism or any other convenient 'ism'. It is much easier to point a finger and accuse the other than to examine oneself – it is so much easier to be the victim. Anne Fine, in her novel *Black Swan*, articulates it well: 'The essence of integrity is wholeness, and wholeness precludes all self-deception, convenient black-outs, the expedient tossing of suddenly inconvenient factors into abeyance.'

To speak of 'something quite rotten at the heart of Catholicism's administration' is not to engage in hyperbole. An excellent example is the comparison of the treatment of Archbishop Bernard Law of Boston and my aforementioned mentor Seán Fagan, the Irish moral theologian. As leader of the Boston Archdiocese, Bernard Law was involved in the cover-up of the behaviour of, and the protection of, a number of abusing priests, five of whom where tried and jailed in 2002. Two of these were particularly notorious, John Geoghan and Paul Shanley. These men were moved around the archdiocese without the parishes being told of their behaviour, which allowed them to abuse children repeatedly. There was no question of Cardinal Law resigning until the trickle of abuse claims became a flood. It was only when a number of the priests of the archdiocese began to call for Law's removal that the Vatican finally accepted his resignation in December 2002, even though he had offered it earlier that year. Following his resignation, Cardinal Law was given the important ceremonial title of Archpriest of St Mary Major in Rome, one of the city's four primary basilicas, the living quarters of which are a magnificent palace.

Fr Seán Fagan, on the other hand, spent his life as a moral theologian: teaching, speaking and writing. He has spent much of his ministry helping people overcome the damage done to them by the church's teaching on sexual matters. He also spoke out strongly on the issue of clerical sexual abuse and placed the responsibility where it belonged, with the hierarchy. In later years he found that he was serving an apostolate to the alienated – those hanging onto Catholicism by their fingertips. He was censured for his book *Does Morality Change?*, though there was little in it that would seem to invite censure. When he produced a second edition of his best-selling work *Has Sin Changed?*, entitled *Whatever Happened to Sin?*, the reaction from the Vatican was swift and brutal. Seán Fagan was forbidden to write, publish, broadcast, give interviews or comment in the public forum. After 50 years of loyal service of priesthood, he was forbidden to do what he did best – to preach the gospel of love. He was neither given the opportunity of due process nor the opportunity to face his accusers. He was also warned that if word of his censure reached the media, even without his co-operation, he would be dismissed from the priesthood.

It is impossible to reconcile the treatment of these two men. This is just one example, but it illustrates the problem perfectly. The man who protected the institution was rewarded; the man who challenged it, based on gospel values, was punished. It was difficult to remain attached to an organisation whose priorities are so skewed. My willingness to remain was little more than homage to my mentor.

Despite my struggle to remain, I find now that I am a dispossessed Catholic. For me the last straw was the Missal translation. This was not an impulsive decision for I have been following the Missal saga since 2000. My objection is not primarily about the language, though that is a constituent part. The new Missal is a product of the bullying and abuse of power that was involved in bringing it about. To stay and participate in using the translation is to collude with the abuses behind it. It is the same bullying that has silenced Seán Fagan and other theologians, and that tried to brow-beat abuse survivors when they first brought their accusations. It is all woven from the same thread – a lust for power and control.

Interestingly, though, the more I disentangle the institutional Catholicism from my faith expressed through Catholicism, for I remain a Catholic, the more it makes sense. The nearness of God, a constant presence in my life, seems ever closer. Lent and Easter have taken on even more powerful meanings. Advent and Christmas have each taken on a completely different focus. My prayer life was never better. My conscience pokes ever more powerfully asking me how I have tended to those marginalised by life and circumstance. It has been a wonderful journey though, even including the bad bits that offered the greatest challenges. Doubt with a capital 'D' has accompanied my faith in adulthood and remains its dark shadow. The deeper my faith becomes, the greater the grip Doubt maintains. I think of Einstein's comment: The greater the circle of light, the greater the circumference of darkness that surrounds it. But I do not worry about Doubt; it saves my faith from becoming a certainty and allows it to remain faith – something I have to affirm anew each day. So when I am asked 'Why do you bother?', the best explanation I have is:

> I would say to myself, 'I will not think about him,
> I will not speak in his name any more,'
> But then there seemed to be a fire burning in my heart,
> imprisoned in my bones.
> The effort to restrain it wearied me,
> I could not do it. (Jeremiah 20:9)

And the fire still burns.

The not-so-secret sayings of Jesus: what the Catholic Church meant and means to me

Peter Costello

To discover what the Catholic Church has meant in my life, I have to go back to the early years of childhood. My family, while Catholic, were not particularly pious in the manner of those days in the early 1950s. However, the Sisters of the Sacred Heart, and a little later the Jesuit Fathers, provided a sort of piety, and in due course the foundations for religious knowledge of a more intellectual kind.

I arrived early then at an interest and concern with religion and with religious matters. This persists. Not all of this interest was in the orthodox, of course. I can still recall the strange thrill with which I surveyed, in Hodges Figgis bookshop, on its publication in 1959, *The Secret Sayings of Jesus* or *The Gospel According to Thomas*. That Christianity had other aspects to it, especially in earlier centuries, than our perennial Irish division into Catholic and Protestant was revealing to the child I was. Did Christianity, seemingly open to all, have secrets known only to a few?

There were other puzzles too. I had an aunt who was married to an Anglican who died about this time from the results of the gassing he had received serving in the Great War. I recall that a neighbouring boy, echoing doubtless something misunderstood over the family breakfast table, asked me 'Do Protestants believe in God?' Nowadays I might well wonder, 'Do Catholics believe in God?' And if so, what kind of God?

Thus we take our tone in so many ways from what surrounds us. I was interested in religion, but often found the religious exercises at school and elsewhere to be confusing and embarrassing. One occasion was not: when we were assembled in our school hall to listen to the radio broadcast, 'direct from Rome', of the burial of Pope Pius XII. That was certainly an impressive, and I now realise, historic occasion. The slow ceremonies, from the coffin being inserted into a series of shells to the final interment, these had a peculiar resonance. It had been a long time since the burial of a Pope, and this was the first such ceremony to be carried out under the observing eye of the modern media, not only of the press and radio, but also television. Little did we realise how these new resources would change our world then, and change the way in which the church was seen and operated.

For with the election of Pope John XXIII – also an important media occasion – the windows in the Vatican were (at least for a time) thrown open and the ecumenical council that followed (by which time I was at a university in the United States) provoked a shift in the tectonic plates of our little world.

The then Archbishop of Dublin and Primate of Ireland, Dr John Charles McQuaid, returned from Rome to reassure his people that all this talk from Rome would not affect the even tenor of their religious customs. Alas, he was wrong, and in any case was too late. He himself, in my opinion, had already done the damage, a decade before there were any hints of an ecumenical council.

Some years ago, in my capacity as the honorary librarian of a Catholic Library, I had to go through a donation of books from a late parish priest in Meath Street. Among the books was a leather bound copy of the 'new catechism' which Dr McQuaid had promoted back in 1952. This was introduced into the schools while I was at the convent: my mother, however, in one of those mix-ups that leave their mark, bought, in Brown and Nolan's, the 'wrong catechism'. She brought home for me another new catechism, which originated in the United States, printed in full colour, a bright little book, which the Diocese of Limerick was promoting. By contrast with the dull pages of the McQuaid volume, with its stiff language and its recycled nineteenth-century German-style illustrations, this was a revelation. Here was a little book in keeping with the style of the modern media, a book for the modern child. It did not last long. Given the influential position of Dr McQuaid, it was soon suppressed. My religious knowledge teacher had to pick and choose among its American answers to find the ones that echoed the Dublin version of the faith. So from an early age, what with secret gospels and wrong catechisms, a different drummer provided the measure of my steps.

However, in this leather bound edition of a familiar book, there was tucked a circular letter from Archbishop McQuaid to the priests of the diocese on the introduction of the Dublin catechism. This was a remarkable document, intended perhaps for 'ours only', as the Jesuits would say. Dr McQuaid sternly counselled the priests that the questions and answers were to be learned by rote. 'No pedagogic theory' was to stand in the way of this. It did not matter, he wrote, if the children did not understand what they were learning at that moment in time; when the children grew into adulthood they would come to an understanding. That this would happen was, of course, a 'pedagogic theory', but different from the novel ones His Grace deprecated, such as those of Maria Montessori, of learning through play. Religion in his view was to be hard work, not fun; a matter of routine, not real interest.

Alas, a generation of Irish children, my generation of Irish children, the so-called 'Baby-Boom' generation, the children too of the dawning age of space, having failed to enculturate the rudiments of their religious knowledge, having failed to interiorise in any way the ancient precepts of the church, at the close of the Council happily threw away their cloak of Catholicism – I exaggerate only a little. Having no knowledge to sustain them, they gave up the faith as a bad job.

We are now living with the consequences. They put away childish things, but not with the consequence the evangelist foresaw; they continued to see darkly rather than face to face. The failure of faith, which so many lament, is I believe not to be laid at the doorstep of 'modern' secular society, or that of the 'modern' media, but at the church's own porch. Behind our present crisis lies a failure of teaching more than half a century ago.

One could see this in the school environment. Many of my friends went to weekly confession. While I was riddled with doubts and hesitations about many aspects of religion, they happily conformed. Come the modernisation of religion, by the 1970s they conformed again. When the country was religious, they were religious: when the country ceased to be religious, they happily ceased to be religious – with a great sense of relief on the half of those erstwhile weekly penitents. Now they felt they had nothing to be penitent about. My doubts lingered on.

So having been a doubtful schoolboy and now a religiously inclined adult, I was once again something of an outsider. Years living in the United States, where there are, so to speak, '57 varieties' of religion also affected my outlook. How could that not be so in a land with nearly every Christian creed you could think of from the Mormons to the Doukhobors (a traditionalist Russian Orthodox sect who were given to protesting naked about government interference in their ways)?

Back in Ireland, the changes were doubtless different in other parts of the country; I am now talking about people who lived and breathed in what would now be characterised as 'Dublin 4' – perhaps not a representative sample.

When I write about 'schoolboy doubts', these may not have been actual doubts, but merely the stirrings of an inquiring mind. One continues to inquire to this day, but these inquiries have taken on a larger dimension.

I acknowledge the Catholic Church as one of the most formative influences on Western civilisation over the last 2,000 years. It has also been important in the creation of what we have of Irish life and culture. It has been important to me as a constant reminder not of certainty but of mystery. For religion is a matter of mystery. The idea that, following the notions of Greek philosophers, we can arrive at certainty in religious matters, seems to me untrue. If we could, religion would not then be a matter of faith. Faith is the accepting that we can be never be certain, but that we can take some things on trust. The gospels persuade us to accept the mysteries they reveal because what they have to say about human matters is so obviously true. The mature Christian learns to live with his/her doubts, indeed may take his/her meaning from them.

So much for what the church has meant. But what of the future? Recent events such as the widespread scandal of clerical child abuse have scarred and scared Catholics of all kinds. For within the church there are many kinds of Catholics, with many kinds of approach to the divine, derived from their own experiences, tastes and emotional inclinations, all legitimate, for there is simply no one way of 'being Catholic'.

But the scandals we know of are, I suspect, as nothing compared with the scandals we as yet know little or nothing of. These have been sexual sins, but other sins, other crimes, especially financial and personal crimes, loom nearer to the Vatican, compared with which the Calvi affair was merely a premonitory symptom, a twitch on a nerve near an ever-growing tumour.

But the crimes we know of, and the crimes we do not know of, do not affect the church as 'the people of God'; these are not the sins of the faithful, but the crimes of the servants of the servants of God; and the gospel speaks coldly of unworthy servants.

The church as an institution will survive, though in ways different from what we have known in the past, or know today. It will, for instance, become less European and there will be few of those over-influential Italian and Spanish clergy in Rome. Indeed, the need for the Pope to be in Rome at all might be questioned, for just as other bishops take their title from cities *in partibus infidelibus*, so the Bishop of Rome does not need to be in his diocese. A future Pope could remove himself to the Far East or to South America.

The church as an institution will continue; what may not continue is the way it is administered. Much of what we see in Rome today is not even as old as the Council of Trent (1545–63). The congregations such as the Congregation for the Doctrine of the Faith are creations of the seventeenth century, an era in which autocratic rulers of France created the first bureaucracies in the world, all the better to rule their people and extract their taxes.

Ironically as the bureaucracies of the church have grown, as is inevitable with bureaucracies, they have become the very image of that 'Big Government' which so many conservative Catholics complain about in the political sphere. Ironically, as the officials have grown, the immediate power of the Pope has been diluted, and the authority of local bishops (which is after all of apostolic origin) has been reduced.

What keeps the Pope in Rome is not a title, but this bureaucracy. Reduce the civil service, increase the immediate authority of the bishops and the teaching prestige of the Pope, and the church will be transformed. 'Let the bishops administer and the Pope teach' might be a watchword for the future. There is no need for His Holiness (or rather his agents) to micromanage the affairs of distant Mayo.

Today in Ireland we witness the strange spectacle of an ever-rising tide of secularism – contested by a minority who tenaciously cling to the comforting ways of their childhood. 'Tradition' is constantly invoked. But this tradition seems to go back only as far as the 1920s, or the Synod of Thurles in 1850, or the Council of Trent. The long laborious centuries of Christianity, especially the first three centuries, are effectively meaningless to many people, who act not out of a creative energy, but out of a deep-seated sense of fear.

But what have they to fear in fact? Instead of invoking tradition and what seems to some (but not all by any means) the essential retention of Latin. But the use of Latin is frivolity in the condition of the present world. This is not the language of Jesus, which was Aramaic; it is not the language of theology, which is Greek; it is the language of lawyers, not pastors. It is a relic of a dead empire, a gift of Caesar the church no longer needs.

It is in any case unfounded in scripture, or so I believe. On that evening when the Holy Spirit descended on the Apostles and the Virgin Mary in the upper room, they were inspired (the women among them too) to go down into the marketplace to preach the Good News, and 'now there were dwelling at Jerusalem, Jews, devout men, out of every nation under heaven … every man [of 15 nations] heard them speak in his own tongue' (Acts 2:6). There is nothing necessary about Latin; it is merely a one-time vernacular that no one now speaks in the marketplaces of the world. And if the work of the church is anywhere, it is in the marketplaces of the world.

All this can be found in Acts 2:1–18. In the light of a more recent controversy it is interesting to read in this first public act of the church, Peter's invocation of Joel: 'I will pour out my Sprit upon all flesh; and your sons and *daughters* shall prophesy … and upon *my handmaids* will I pour out in those days of my spir-it' – all of which seems to give an emphatic, prominent and equal role to women in the service of the church. (These quotes are from the Rheims version of 1582; not, I know, a scholarly source by today's norms, but I am afraid old habits die hard.)

Others call for a return to liturgical formality, to a liturgy that others say demands more priests than we will ever have again – now that in Ireland at least Catholic mothers are resolutely persuading their sons against the priesthood.

We need to go back to the source of that tradition: the words of Christ in the gospels. We need to espouse a sense of the smaller Christian community, happily living among a larger society, anxious to share its insights with others, but reluctant to impose them, especially not through the services of the state. We cannot make people good by referendum. We are commanded to render unto God the things that are God's, and unto Caesar the things that are Caesar's. In this we have nothing to fear, save fear itself.

But above all this, as the decades have advanced and the church remains lumbered with the machinery of governance which no longer works, and which is clogging up on petty detail, as 'a child of the space age' I have grown ever more conscious of where we really are in space and time.

Man's antiquity now stretches away into a million years or more; the universe itself, whatever its origins, into an unimagined age and an unimaginable size. The last 2,000 years are almost nothing in the timescale we now have before us.

Even if we reduce man's history to a mere half million years, one has to ask where was God then. He was there of course, for the earliest signs of humanity already reveal a belief in the spirit, and already reveal religion at work. Those millennia of 'natural religion' are also a part of revelation. So too the awe-inspiring fact that so very few of the human race in the long course of history have been Christian. We have to come to terms with that, but again this is one of the mysteries of religion. Pascal, the seventeenth-century philosopher (1623–62), observed that the 'eternal silence of those infinite spaces' terrified him. They do not terrify me so much. They leave me in awe, for they are not truly silent, but in their very appearance, their very existence, they convey a message, a revelation even, of the great creative mind.

Teilhard de Chardin speculated that beyond the evolution of man's physical form, his mind, his spirit, was also evolving, that just as our knowledge over the centuries has increased, so in some ways our spiritual natures have been enlarging, that in this 'noosphere' (a spiritual counterpart to the biosphere) we are moving ever nearer, but slowly, to an 'Omega point', which will involve a completion of our knowledge of the divine.

It was an idea that seemed to many of his admirers to greatly enlarge our view of man's place in nature. But Teilhard was also deeply aware, in ways very hard to communicate, of dimensions to the incarnation, of what was fully implied in Christ becoming Man that transcended the simpler notions of our childhood catechism.

But for most Christians, simpler notions must serve in everyday life. I once wondered, as *The Gospel of Thomas* implies, if Christianity, seemingly open to all, had secrets known only to a few?

No, is now the answer. For, as I suggest, we ought as Christians to return to the source of our tradition, to the veridical gospels. There an authentic voice speaks, thankfully not in the tones of the professional theologian, or of the Vatican apparatchik, but in terms of the great simplicity. It is no longer a matter of 'the secret sayings of Jesus', but of the authentic teachings of Christ. It is no longer a matter of 'the wrong catechism'. There is no secret at the heart of Christianity known only to a few; it is all an open book, open to all who can read, or hear.

'What then must a man do?' that irregular Christian Leo Tolstoy once asked rhetorically. The answer is in the gospels: we must worship God and love our neighbour as ourselves. That is the essence of it all, except that we must all learn to be as charitable and forgiving as Jesus was, to seek out the Samaritans among us and the Gentiles beyond us. Those far-from-secret sayings of Jesus, that 'in my father's house there are many mansions' (John 14:2) and that 'other sheep I have that are not of this fold' (John 10:16) are I think to be taken quite literally – they imply an evolving relationship with the world's other religions, with the cosmos itself, indeed with what we mean by 'truth', which we have hardly begun to explore, let alone understand.

All the answers then are in the source of our tradition, in the pages of the gospels. The church has to return not upon its own recent teachings, not upon theology, or on the canons of the church, but upon *the source* of those teachings, those beliefs, those rules, acting always in the deepest spirit of *caritas*. Whatever about learning the catechism by rote, this will be really hard work. The next million years will be interesting.

What we must do is respond to that child's voice in the street, at one of the most significant moments in the life of a great saint, as if it were a voice from our own childhood years: *Tolle, lege.*

Where I stand with my Catholicism

Angela Macnamara

The potential pain of change, any change, must never be under-estimated. The change in the Catholic Church since I was a child pre-Vatican II, has been no less than a spiritual and cultural upheaval. Many Catholics can no longer find their way, caught in what seems like a dense fog. For some people change is a 'little death'. The young, little taught and inexperienced in terms of faith, make their own giddy route, calling it 'freedom' but, in truth, unable to anticipate the mist-shrouded pitfalls. Others, by grace and openness, discern the Spirit of God in the darkness.

I was born in October 1931 the second daughter of George Little and Alice Mulhern Little. My father was a doctor practis-ing on Rathgar Road, Dublin. I started life in middle-class comfort.

It was my mother who introduced us to a loving, merciful God with whom she had a strong personal relationship. She nurtured our faith and dedicated herself to family care and home responsibilities. I was a delicate, asthmatic child and spent a lot of time home from school in my early years. I was never an intel-lectual, but was creative and canny in an instinctual way. My mother influenced me to find comfort and healing in my devel-oping relationship with Jesus, my 'invisible companion'.

Things changed for us all when I was about 10 years old and my father became ill with heart trouble. His periods of poor health brought extra worry and responsibility to Mother. From then on, for years, she drove him on his morning rounds and generally kept a concerned eye on his way of life. I was anxious about both of them.

My sister and I attended school at the Convent of the Sacred Heart, Leeson Street, Dublin where we were very happy. The Sisters were devoted to their pupils. There was no such thing as corporal punishment either in school or at home. When I was about 13 a teacher commented that I 'would always be a maverick'. I didn't mention this at home because I wasn't sure that it was a good thing. I went on to become Head Girl of the school in 1948.

With a view to becoming a journalist, I studied for a year at a commercial college. Being offered a job in the medical secretary's office in the National Maternity Hospital as soon as I had finished the commercial course, I happily took up that position. There, I was further educated in 'the facts of life'.

At the age of 21 I got engaged to Peter Macnamara who was a chartered engineer. We married in May 1953.

By 1960 four beautiful daughters had arrived. I was writing a monthly article in the *Messenger of the Sacred Heart*. It occurred to me then that I had plunged into marriage, like a significant number of girls in that era, without any useful inside information on marriage, childbearing and parenting.

That resulted in my idea that I would write down all that I felt should be shared with girls in senior classes and try and find a school principal who would take the idea on board and, possibly, along with it, take me to do the job.

I succeeded immediately in finding a religious sister at a local school who, after time and consultation with her staff, agreed to have me. Thus began over 20 years of talks in schools throughout the country. As time passed, I spoke in a few boys' schools and, at my insistence, with parents and teachers. The age of greatest need moved down to sixth class in primary schools.

In 1962 I wrote six articles on my findings in the schools and these were published in *The Sunday Press* over six Sundays. The response in terms of letters to me, was so significant that Frank Carty (the then editor) decided to keep the column going until the flow of letters dried up. Thus I became an agony aunt for 18 years as well as continuing with the schools' work. The official church did not encourage me for many years. I was inadvertently opening a Pandora's box. Later, but almost too late, I got a tentative approval.

At that time, there was a wind of change blowing through the whole of Irish society. From a closed, insular Catholic country, we were spreading our nets to catch all the popular culture that the UK and the USA were advertising. Means of communication were letting us know about a new world beyond our shores – more freedom, more excitement, new methods of communication.

The Catholic Church needed to state its position afresh, and get rid of extraneous rules and regulations and arrogant attitudes which had worked for a timid, unquestioning people of bygone days. The church was called then, and more so as the years passed, to speak in a language understandable to ordinary people. (Words such as 'transubstantiation' and 'consubstantial' are for the academic world.) 'Now is the hour of the laity' (Pope John Paul II). But the church was a slowly awakening giant, feeling powerful and triumphant.

Instead of having arrived, the church today is 'becoming', groaning in the birthing of Christianity, and begging for forgiveness for failures. Old ways must give way to the new. Ways of 'being' – authority, secrecy, 'obligations', indulgences, penitential exercises, a plethora of novenas and devotions, paying for Masses, superiority of men, sexuality, under-rating of women, the value of celibacy, schools, power and grandeur – all of these come into the list of required changes in the church. Overbearing authority alienates and creates anger and anxiety. Successful leadership is differently understood today. It entails moral authority with an understanding as to how best to encourage and inspire. It listens to the faithful and to other churches, and interprets with humility and love rather than imposing excessive control. Christian unity is a priority.

For too long grandeur in dress, a wealthy style of living, intolerance, angling for position and other unsavoury attitudes around money and ways of being, have been associated with the Vatican. By baptism we are called to be saints. The leadership of the church no longer convinces me of that truth. Perhaps I say that because the messages of the Pope do not percolate through to the Sunday homily? I feel angry at the absence of leadership for myself, my children and grandchildren.

Christian conversion is not found in an accumulation of dictates but in hearts that are warmly touched by the positive teaching of a merciful God through Jesus and inspired by the Holy Spirit. I must say that I favour the beatitudes to the commandments of the church as taught in my day.

I believe that it takes men, along with women, to interpret, prayerfully and with contemplation, what God wants of God's people. Christian conversion is a matter of seeking union with God and we need to learn that.

Celibacy is the way some may choose to achieve this goal. Amongst those I respect greatly as convinced celibates is the Curé d'Ars (John Vianney). He is one of those special people who showed an 'overmastering passion' for God. What I perceive to have happened in Ireland decades ago is that the idealistic young man encouraged by parents, spurred on by priest teachers, accepted celibacy as a given. But when faced by age and the experience of real human needs, some found that 'it is not good that man should be alone'.

It seems to be counter-productive in our times to close seminarians off from their fellow students by way of locked doors. Christ mixed freely with men and women. When a troubled man, not yet a saint, finds himself without a human helpmate, he seeks a friend in whom he can confide. Naturally it will often be a woman because of the God-given nature of men and women. Likewise have we seen celibate women seek to confide in priests and, either way, the unexpected sexual dynamism can open their eyes. That may be a positive experience in which celibacy is maturely and prayerfully re-affirmed or re-considered. Hence my belief is in optional celibacy for the priesthood. To have married priests seems to me to be a healthy alternative. (I do not underestimate the logistical problems in such change. But this is not the place for discussion of these issues.)

The old word 'matrimony' seems to reflect the outdated teaching of the church on sexuality. The church needs to have a total review of its teaching on relationships and sexuality. At present its teaching is irrelevant to the majority of people. It seems that extra-marital sex, co-habitation for couples who are committed to each other, contraception, abortion, divorce and the Eucharist for divorced people in new relationships, need to have a new light shone on them. As it is, people make their own decisions. An 'anything goes' mentality has taken over even for the most well-intentioned people. The 'now' generation has simply written off the church as an influential institution speaking to us *in persona Christi* (in the person of Christ). Many people do not even know Christ.

This brings us to have a look at what is happening to Christian and, more specifically, Catholic education. This situation is a real 'hot potato' for the church and for Catholic parents and teachers. Is Catholic education accurately defined? Can non-practising, nominally Catholic teachers deliver the sort of Catholic education given by the devoted Catholic? Is there a reasonable definition of what the 'mores' of the Catholic school might be? The fact that approximately one-third of the pupils in some urban primary schools are foreign nationals and speak little English presents enormous problems. This is particularly so where cutbacks already limit the number of teachers and the amount of space available. Watching over the basic, happy integration of these children and ensuring that they are not bullied, is already a tough demand. Most teachers are over-worked and frustrated by state and church.

Secondary schools have a whole raft of difficulties of their own in designing a programme for teaching religious faith where there are groups of notoriously apathetic and anti-establishment adolescents. Significant numbers of parents have lost their sense of religion.

The remaining parents who want their children taught the faith must be prepared to help out in faith-based programmes for themselves and for their children. Heretofore the transmission of the faith was often left completely to religious sisters, priests and religious brothers. Now the Christian home will have to become a place where love, respect, forgiveness, charity, sobriety and, not least, prayer will be the required values that are lived daily. 'See these Christians, how they love one another' (Tertullian). Encouraging programmes need to be initiated.

While the argument for confirmation will continue to be made in primary school, I believe that pupils should opt personally for confirmation after the age of 14. This presupposes parish-based religious instruction and discussions for parents and pupils. Such presentations would be available to people who have personally chosen to be confirmed.

Sunday Masses might become beacons for the week, better understood and anticipated with joy by priests and people if, instead of having Mass available every weekday – attended mostly by retired people who feel happy with the *status quo* – there might be a variety of ongoing instructions in the faith. Films, reflections, readings and discussions, could be made available around, perhaps, 10–11 a.m. and again at a suitable hour in the evening time, three days per week followed by Holy Communion using pre-sanctified Hosts. Funeral Masses, of course, take precedence when they occur. Priests need to become more proficient in modern communications skills (not gimmicks) for use in preaching the gospel. Teams of selected, trained lay people could help (not just from the 'Yes Father, No Father' group). Otherwise where do the faithful receive their ongoing religious education? With fewer Masses and more instruction, the sacrifice of the Mass might be presented with more enthusiasm. Readings might be prepared carefully during the week, and explained and read with clarity. The Eucharist needs to have its intrinsic value reiterated. Talking in the church after Mass should be disallowed to show respect for those who wish to continue their thanksgiving and adoration.

The idea of Masses for the deceased being paid for, some priests insist, at a minimum of €10.00 per Mass, is distasteful to me. Why, having had the funeral Mass for which the celebrant is given the due stipend, should we have further Masses said for the deceased? That was not always the way in the church. Don't we all pray publicly and privately during every Mass, and at other times, for loved ones who have died and ask God's comfort for the relatives?

Many people prefer the service of reconciliation before Christmas and Easter to the private confession in a confessional. Others argue that their confession is made as part of the Mass anyway ('I confess …'). Priests cannot be expected to be qualified counsellors but to be *alter Christus* (other Christ) conveying his mercy and understanding. Thoughtful penances would be appreciated.

It is a sign of our stressed times that the material needs and wants of the church often get discussed before the subject of prayer is explained or mastered. Even theological expertise does not necessarily make a person effective in prayer or desiring with all his/her heart to mediate God's love, mercy, forgiveness and understanding to the whole world. This is basic to evangelisation. We must search to show people that the Good News really is Good News, not merely a dull cliché which people have heard innumerable times. To be able to live our lives knowingly in the presence of God is what matters most. We share this by being with another in their difficulty and pain. I am reminded of the words of Francis Thompson, 'Ah, fondest, blindest, weakest, I am he whom thou seekest ...'

Of course we are not 'hit' by an instant, lasting gift of closeness to God. Fr John Dalrymple quotes T.S. Eliot: 'We are given brief moments of fusion with God which transform us, but they are only moments', before concluding:

'... and the rest
Is prayer, observance, discipline, thought
And action.'

For most of the time we try to absorb the messages of scripture and struggle with selfishness, human frailty and oft times with the shadow of disbelief. It is in a moment of special grace that the inclination to talk with God – to pray – is born.

Prayers learned by heart can be a great help in arid moments. Recited slowly, they can take on new depth and meaning. I believe in holy pictures in the home. Just as a framed photograph of a child reminds me to communicate with a child who is abroad, so the tasteful representation of the Holy reminds me to turn my heart in that blessed direction.

Who have we to make the scriptures sing for us? We long for joy, for God who comes 'leaping over the mountains, skipping across the hills' as the psalmist describes it. There are priests out there whose selflessness, warm demeanour, down-to-earth holiness and joy touch hearts daily. We must pray for an increase in their numbers and, whoever we are, join with them when we can. The Holy Spirit is with us. Priests and faithful will arise and go forward on the power of God to build the broken reality. We have today a humbled and vibrant church.

The changing score of Catholicism

Bernadette Flanagan

In my office the picture *Lost in Motion* by the Dutch artist Kitty Meijering hangs on the wall. The whirring white lines of motion in the picture convey the rapid movement of the dancer. The expression on the dancer's face indicates that her movement is not tedious or studied, but rather emanates her sympathetic responsiveness to the music that she is hearing. The picture symbolically represents that life may be a call to move creatively with the music that plays in the background. This image shapes the narrative of what you are about to read.

The first movement of the dance is set in Walsh Island, County Offaly. How can a place that is far from the sea have such an enigmatic name? Well, the water that surrounds the 'island' where I grew up is held in the sodden earth of the Bog of Allen peat-lands. But the name of this village may now attract attention for reasons other than its puzzling islandic reference. In particular, the Ryan Report dealt with the case of the paedophile Offaly teacher Donal Dunne, who is referred to in the Report by the pseudonym of 'John Brander'. He was convicted for the sexual abuse of boys at Walsh Island National School, where he was the principal teacher. His period in Walsh Island, from 1966 to 1969, also led to complaints from 11 female pupils of violent punishments. Witnesses told the Ryan Commission of reluctance by parents to challenge Donal Dunne, since Dunne's brother-in-law was a foreman in a local business, and many of his pupils' fathers were employed by his relation, leading to an unwillingness to complain.

During Donal Dunne's time in Walsh Island I was in second, third and fourth class. These classes had two female teachers. His wife taught junior and senior infants and needlecraft to other classes. These three female teachers participated in the preparation for confirmation for which Donal Dunne was in charge, and I personally was present at scenes where these teachers witnessed the 'violent punishments'. In particular, I recall how the inability to remember the Benediction response *'Omne delectamentum in se habentem'* (Having in itself all delight) provoked his great ire. The fact that my preparation for confirmation was under the tuition of Donal Dunne captures some of the strange cadences which the blend of Catholicism and biography create in my lifestory.

The Ryan Report also profiles the abuse of residents at St Conleth's Reformatory, Daingean, County Offaly (1940–73). The fear and intimidation that the report describes was not however confined within its walls. 'Daingean' was a symbol in the language of leading adults in Walsh Island (just five miles from Daingean) which used to incite fear and trembling in anyone threatened to be dispatched to its enclosures. Here again, I had a direct encounter with the ambiguity of Irish Catholic identity. In particular, I was learning how the work for justice that was strong in the religious magazines that were part of the Catholic environment of my childhood, such as *The Far East*, did not extend to challenging local manifestations of deficits in compassion.

The second movement of the narrative of my relationship with Catholicism takes place in Dungarvan, County Waterford, where I was a boarder at the Presentation Secondary School (1971–6). Here the blend of Catholicism and biography assumes a faster, more exciting melody. It was in this place that I had my first encounter with Catholic feminism in action – though it might not have had that name back then. It was clear that the girls studying in this school were preparing to have lives quite different from our mothers, most of whom had been full-time homemakers, due in part to the marriage bar still in place up to the 1960s. Career guidance was provided and our minds were opened to the diverse possibilities beyond teaching and nursing to which women could aspire in the 1970s. When practical blocks, like lack of access to honours mathematics and other science subjects, stood in the way of such aspirations, no stone was left unturned to remove these barriers, including collaborating with the local boys' secondary school. The religious sisters in the community went back to college to gain further qualifications so as to ensure the sustained availability of new languages and the science subjects. The changing style of women's religious life unfolded before our eyes as hemlines shortened and clothes became less restrictive in their style. The walls were tumbling and the driving lessons being taken by members of the community pointed symbolically to the new visionary horizons being embraced by this group of sisters. Catholicism and the empowerment of women were twinned in my mind in this experience.

It was not unusual therefore that I opted to become part of this exciting movement and so joined the community after finishing in secondary school. My best friend also joined the group in her home town with the hope of working for the empowerment of women in Pakistan. Though getting to Pakistan did not happen immediately for her, she has now spent 20 happy years there. Catholicism and my personal biography thus became fused in a very concrete form, though this was not to the fore in my thoughts when I joined the Presentation Sisters in 1976.

In this life choice the music moved from the mid-paced gavotte to a fast-moving sherzo. Three months after joining the community, changes happened arising from the call of Vatican II to religious communities to reignite the charismatic spirit of those who founded the communities. The training for new members became internationalised and I joined a group where Irish, English, Filipino and Zimbabwean sought together to understand how the vision and spirit of the eighteenth-century innovative, dynamic Cork woman, Nano Nagle, might be translated into different cultural settings, according to the call of the signs of the times. Global Catholicism was experienced firsthand and it provided a wider perspective on the local Irish expression of Catholicism that had been inherited through growing up in Ireland. These women might become the only face of Catholicism in remote regions of the world or be martyred for their service to the poor and excluded. In such a setting our focus had to be turned inward like the dancer so as to learn how to be attuned to those resources within each of us that would enable us to respond with enduring resilience to the ever-unfolding music of the dance in our diverse locations.

In learning these skills of inward attunement in the midst of sometimes intense external pressures and noise, spiritual guidance by Patrick Cusack SJ was invaluable. His aphorism 'muddied waters, allowed stand, become clear', with its Taoist resonances, when blended with his persistent biblical message 'be still and know that I am God' (Psalm 46:10) was an introduction to what today might be called 'mindfulness', long before such a practice became so widely appreciated. The centrality of spiritual practice to the way of life being chosen, as well as a raised awareness of the resources within Catholicism for developing such a practice, made a deep impression on me in these two years of training.

After training, life moved back towards the mid-pace of a gavotte again. A unique encounter with the public structures of Catholicism in Ireland marked this phase as I was part of a new programme launched by the Pontifical University in Maynooth to open the study of theology to persons other than clerical students. The 'BA Theol', as the programme was known, uniquely cracked a stained-glass ceiling in Ireland for women. This was the foundation programme from which numerous women – Linda Hogan, Sue Mulligan, Máire Byrne, Olive Cullen – have gone on to gain doctorates in a field of study from which they had been excluded up to that time. The professors who taught on the programme enjoyed the enthusiasm of students taking theology by academic choice, rather than as a prerequisite for ordination. In my own case the encouragement of Revd Prof. Tom Marsh RIP and Revd Prof. Patrick Hannon were critical to opening up the vista of doctoral studies to me. Their support was of course tinted with the ambiguity of being encouraged to become equipped to participate in the provision of theological education, though the presence of women in such Catholic settings was virtually unknown.

In due course postgraduate studies were completed and the unique challenges of finding employment in the family business of Irish Catholicism were encountered. The fact that Catholic theological studies have been co-located in centres which prepared men for the priesthood – Maynooth, Kimmage Manor, Milltown Institute and All Hallows College – was central to the ambiguity encountered. How could those who had not passed through the phases and stages of clerical studies be equipped to teach clerics in the classroom, even if one had a PhD in a theological specialisation?

There were other ambiguities to be navigated in these environments. Those who were ordained could perform multiple roles simultaneously – academic, chaplain to a service, priest in a parish. Employment contracts were shaped to accommodate such multiple realities. How then could a contract be negotiated if one were to practise solely as an academic? Inevitably, this meant that administration roles would fill the equivalent of priestly duties. The differences between an academic employment environment designed by women with women for women, as had been experienced in Dungarvan, and an employment environment rooted in the clerical roles in Catholicism came into sharp relief. Since the teaching of theology had not, for historical reasons, become embedded in the Irish university system, the influence of public employment protocols which might contribute to the identification of viable career paths for the non-ordained was not relevant.

In the midst of these challenges, the blending of the role of academic manager with spirituality scholar opened new vistas. In particular, it was possible through handling application enquiries to become familiar with the heart and mind of those who make applications to centres for the study of religion in Ireland. What became undeniably evident was the deep interest in matters of the soul, in the personal spiritual journey, in the contours of spiritual awakening and in the heritage of mystical writings that Catholicism holds, which was awakening. My dual role employed my academic skills to conceive the contours of programmes in spirituality and my management skills to lead a team in designing and accrediting such programmes. In these years (2001–7) I saw the numbers undertaking spirituality studies rise exponentially. The convictions of the German Jesuit theologian Karl Rahner that the Christian of the future would be a mystic or be nothing at all, and of the Fordham University Professor Ewert Cousin that humanity was entering the second axial period of spiritual consciousness, were unfolding in living form before my eyes.

Ultimately, an institutional readiness for the turn to spirituality was not in place. It has always been the case that mystics can provoke unease and so it is not totally surprising that educational programmes that would empower post-conventional religious development would run into difficulties. Catholicism in Ireland faces innumerable challenges at this time – maybe even an unprecedented crisis. In the hundreds of conversations that I have had with the Irish public through my involvement in the academic study of spirituality over the past 15 years, I am convinced that Ireland is passing through a spiritual transition. As Christopher Fry has so aptly indicated, 'affairs are now soul-size'.

In order to address this hunger I have now developed an alternative approach beyond the academy. I have found that a new global expression of the spiritual quest variously entitled 'new monasticism', 'monasticism without walls', 'everyday monasticism' and 'portable monasticism' has the structure and foundations to support the quest for spiritual practice in daily life settings. The image of a monk works at an archetypal level. It evokes the passionate commitment to Christian discipleship that drove the first Christian monastics into the Egyptian and Syrian desert; it echoes the relentless energy of the early Irish monks wrestling with the great waves in small boats and it recalls images of great spiritual teachers such as Br Roger of Taizé and Thomas Merton from the contemporary era. In the apostolic letter issued by John Paul II at the opening of the third millennium – *Novo millienio ineunte* (*At the beginning of the new millennium*) – there is a sympathetic recognition that unless the disciple of the future lives with the spiritual attunement of Jesus, then the traditional expressions of discipleship may become empty activism, masks of the gospel rather than its true expression. In the end it seems Catholicism and I are synchronised to a hidden music where the dancer and the dance embrace.

Bring flowers of the rarest

Gay Mitchell

As a boy I believe I heard the gospel passage read as 'In my Father's house there are many mansions' (John 14:2). I feel sure that there are rooms there for Catholics, other Christians, Muslims, Jews, Hindus and non-believers. For some reason I was born into a Catholic family, though my paternal grandfather was Methodist, and I inherited my, sometimes weak, faith from my mother.

My family has had much good fortune and throughout the marriages, baptisms and celebrations, church was always in the background. My family has also had much tragedy: my parents' first son, my brother Patrick, aged 15, was killed on a midsummer's day in a bicycle accident. Their first daughter, my sister Hazel, was discovered to be what we used to call mentally handicapped when she was four, presumed to be because of pressure on her brain at birth.

My parents adopted two more children and then, when my mother was aged 47, my father died of cancer, leaving her with nine young children. My mother had a daily prayer routine that kept her going and to this day I keep her prayer book in my bedroom. She was a devout person but was broad-minded and tolerant. In later years, two of my brothers and a sister died of the same curse of cancer at an average age of 49. Throughout all of these tragedies, the rites of the Catholic Church brought us great consolation.

I visited New Zealand in the early 1980s and I recall reading there that, for a successful life, Maoris believe we need love, prayer and ritual. Most people probably identify with love and prayer. Ritual is important too. My experience is that the rites of the Catholic Church bring hope, consolation and meaning to life.

Sceptics might well ask 'How could Jesus rise from the dead?' Coming alive again has to be a real possibility since we came alive in the first place. What I find hardest to believe is that he went through such awful pain and suffering for sinners, and not for the righteous. His resurrection is a central teaching of the Christian religion. In the Catholic tradition, there is a very special rite that Jesus left behind and is available to the church's members, all of us sinners, that peace that Jesus said he was leaving us. I sometimes wonder what other Christian churches make of those words: 'Whose sins you shall forgive they are forgiven, whose sins you shall retain they are retained' (John 20:23).

I once visited the Church of the Holy Sepulchre in Jerusalem, the believed burial place of Christ. It was an extraordinary experience. I tried to sense that Jesus was once actually present there. One of the priests in charge of the Sepulchre told me that one can get the sense of real presence in any Catholic church throughout the world. I believe he is right. One of the things that makes the Roman Catholic denomination different from many other Christian denominations and religious sects is the belief in the Real Presence of Jesus in the Eucharist.

To be a Christian, one must believe in the resurrection. To be a Roman Catholic, one also has to believe in the consecration of bread and wine at Mass (the Real Presence). Being present at Mass to share in this is a great privilege and gift. I have never in my life found it difficult to go to Mass.

In Lutheran and Anglican churches, the respectful atmosphere and the peace and quiet are indeed conducive to prayer. However, in my experience, universally, there is an extra dimension in a Catholic church, the Real Presence of Christ in the Eucharist. A house that feels more like a home.

In *What Makes Us Catholic*, Thomas Groome advises that we should proceed with caution when approaching the term 'identity' in any religion. He nonetheless states that a conspicuous feature of Catholic Christianity is how symbol-laden it is, myriad symbols that nurture identity. He is right on both counts. Symbols are important for Catholics: the crucifix, the shamrock, Ash Wednesday and holy water come to mind. So are dates, not just the ones all Christians observe but others: November, the month of the Holy Souls, and May, the month of Mary.

The grotto replica of Lourdes at the Oblate Fathers, Inchicore, Dublin is a really special place of prayer. Having grown up beside that hallowed place, where the annual May procession was a community occasion, the Marian hymn *Bring Flowers of the Rarest* still stirs my emotions.

The reported words of Our Lady at Lourdes, humbly asking Bernadette if she would do her the favour of visiting that place a number of times, ring true. How well those words fit with the biblical admonition to act justly, love tenderly and walk humbly in the ways of the Lord (Micah 6:8). The central place of the Virgin Mary in the rituals of the Catholic Church distinguishes it signally from some other Christian traditions. I am very much at home with this.

I'm not good with feast days, but I always remember 8 December, the Feast of the Immaculate Conception. When I was a very young boy, Catherine Delaney, a friend of my mother, used to visit our home regularly. On 8 December she always celebrated her Christmas Day; it was the highlight of her year. She felt that the Mother of Jesus was not remembered sufficiently on Christmas Day. Mrs Delaney was found dead lying on her bed with a smile on her face on 8 December. Have we become so cool that we dismiss events like that as mere coincidence? I hope not.

The gifts of the Holy Spirit are awe, wonder, wisdom, understanding, fortitude, good judgement and reverence. Awe and wonder are childlike, not childish, qualities. Some of the most extraordinary people I have met in public life, business and religion have this quality in abundance. It is childlike to believe in miracles, but miracles do happen. Was not, for example, the fall of the Berlin Wall a truly miraculous occurrence? I do believe in the miraculous and the Bible says there are angels. Sometimes I wonder if near misses I have had were attributable to the intervention of my guardian angel, to whom I still say a prayer each morning.

Frederic Ozanam died in 1853, aged 40. He was a French scholar and at age 20 one of the founders of the Society of St Vincent de Paul, now present in over 130 countries. This teaches that every person can make a real difference, no matter how short his or her life. The Oblate Fathers supported a St Vincent de Paul Boys' Club, St Josephs', Inchicore, of which I became a member. There I was introduced to the plays of Boucicault, Lady Gregory, Sean O'Casey and John B. Keane. The only part I had in a play was that of the murdered visitor in *The Field*. Musicals were an annual event and to this day I enjoy Gilbert and Sullivan operetta.

I became a youth leader and later treasurer and then President of the St Vincent de Paul Council for Youth Clubs. The Council had 20 youth clubs in Dublin, one of which was St Paul's in Artane. Norma (whom I later married) was a youth leader there, that's how I met her. We were taught that no act of charity is foreign to the Society and Norma remains a member of the organisation to this day. The role of women in the church should not be confined to these acts of charity.

I really cannot understand why the church I am a lifelong member of does not ordain women or allow priest to get married (other than those who joined as married priests from the Anglican tradition).

There are times when I have found the Roman Catholic Church to be too harsh, too rules-driven, certain to the point of arrogance, intrusive and even bullying. But I also remember a church that ran schools without which the poorest, in particular, would never have received an education. A church that managed hospitals and provided physical, as well as spiritual, aid when a fledgling state was not able to do so. A church where men and women dedicated themselves to the service of others at home and in the Third World, out of belief.

I somehow naturally rebel against titles like Eminence, Grace and Lordship, and I really am not at ease with a male-dominated church. At the same time I believe in good order, continuity and the pursuit of truth. I appreciate the well-argued case of Pope Benedict XVI on the dangers of relativism. We cannot decide right and wrong on a show of hands; some things are right or wrong in essence. A church cannot be all things to all people. The fact that the Roman Catholic Church has a central teaching authority, has the Holy Father at its head and tries, though it has erred many times down through the centuries, to pursue truth, is, in my view, central to the handing on of the Christian tradition.

Supposing there was no Roman Catholic Church. If we had a series of national churches, or, say, a multiple of small Christian sects, wouldn't it be very easy for the Christian message to become diluted and lost? If there was not the Roman Catholic Church would other churches, even those who protest about its errant ways, be lost for a standard against which to measure their own beliefs? Would Catholics themselves be without an authentic framework in which to exercise their free will in an informed way? If there was no Roman Catholic Church would something similar have to be created?

In my youth, monthly sodality was the norm, organised separately for boys, men, girls and women. I still remember most of the words of *Tantum Ergo*. I wonder did anyone other than the priest know what they meant? Still, chanting has its place in most religions. I was an altar boy as the era of the Latin Mass was coming to an end. Just after the consecration there would be a collective clearing of throats, the whole service was done by rote and coughing was just one more collective act. We have come a long way, but our journey must continue. History teaches that the Catholic Church itself must be constantly recreated and reinvigorated if it is not to regress.

On becoming Archbishop of Dublin, Diarmuid Martin said that the church must find new ways of evangelising. Yes, the church must learn new ways of spreading the gospel, but also new ways of spreading information about its role, its social conscience and its leaders. I wonder did it ever occur to the Catholic bishops that they might encourage the recruitment of the services of journalists who would put together a weekly newspaper with a Christian ethos, perhaps as a co-operative venture? Not a religious newspaper but a newspaper informed by Christian values. This might even be funded by voluntary subscription recruited through parish outlets throughout the country. The editor of a new newspaper (now there's a job I'd love) would have to be given a clear mandate, but the example of the editorial freedom of *The Irish Times* could be followed – albeit with a different ethos, campaigning on social issues such as the sanctity of life, and ethical economics. Wouldn't it be marvellous to have a newspaper which, for example, campaigned to put 'social' back in the social market economy, as the Catholic bishops of Europe, through their organisation COMECE, advocate? The church is in the business of communicating a message; why not communicate in this way? The media has a very powerful influence, Christians and like-minded others need their voice to be heard.

I believe in the principle of 'live and let live'. I respect others and I want to share this country and continent with them by celebrating diversity. Roman Catholics are part of that diversity; increasingly I feel the need to ensure that there is awareness of this.

I attended Mass recently in La Paz, Bolivia. The large numbers attending were awesome to behold. I was at Holy Thursday Mass in Lima, Peru on the way home; it was the same. I have attended Masses in Rwanda and Mali. The hope and happiness that church life brings to the humble of heart in these countries is striking.

In my view, one of the strongest attractions of Catholicism is its efforts to keep alive the gospel message without making it all things to all people. Yet, I find myself attracted to the Anglican tradition of synods of the clergy and laity where issues of doctrine, and related matters, are debated.

The Catholic Church has much more support, and many more admirers, than is evident from public commentary. The pity is that there is no real forum for the laity to make an effective input, and take our share of responsibility, in a way that is real, effective and valued. Perhaps it is time to borrow from the Anglican tradition and hold an annual synod of lay and clerical Catholics to help fill this vacuum. Bishops, priests and laity could learn much from the humble of heart. Collectively we are the church; all Catholics must take a share of the responsibility if the church we belong to and love is to be reinvigorated.

Keeping faith

Mairead McGuinness

Faith is important to me. It always was and I expect it always will be. Faith is one of those intangible things, beyond religious belief and deeply personal. Faith is a bedrock for me and a bulwark in difficult times.

I am a Catholic, born in 1959 into a Catholic family, at a time when religious ritual and routine were a major part of the daily lives of Irish Catholics. My parents married in 1954 and had five children in quick succession – not unusual in the Ireland of the 1950s. A fire destroyed our home in 1960 and resulted in a small gap in the family but, when some normality was restored after the terrible loss of house and possessions, three more children were born.

Like my seven siblings, I was baptised, received Holy Communion, was confirmed and married in the Catholic tradition. My parents, now sadly both deceased, were also from Catholic families and continued the traditions in which they were brought up, handing them on to us as best they knew how.

When asked to write about Catholicism and what it means to me, I was brought back in time to think about my awareness of Catholicism and what impact being a Catholic had on me as a child. There was no possibility of choosing one's faith, but for those of us born Catholic there comes a time – maybe several times along life's path – when we are forced or required to think about our faith and our church.

One of my earliest memories of childhood, Catholicism and faith is of walking in various religious processions through the streets of Ardee, County Louth, my home town. The May procession dedicated to the Blessed Virgin Mary is particularly memorable, as are the traditions of the May altar in the house and the sounds of the traditional hymns sung as we walked the main street. An immense sense of belonging, pride and occasion remains with me to this day.

Back then, my world was very small – I recall once believing that Ardee was an island! Trips to Dublin were major events. Our world was insular, secure and closeted.

A less happy memory of Catholicism is the sense of fear that surrounded some of the religious events, especially preparing for First Confession. I can recall vividly the gripping fear of stepping into that dark wooden confessional box with the forbidding curtained small grid opening between child and priest.

As I write, I can recall the sound of the sliding door and the face of the priest through the shadowy grid as I half kneeled and half stood up to begin my confessional ritual. I am not sure which was most terrifying, the fear of the dark or the fear of what the priest might say on hearing my four sins. These were to become the perennial four I juggled for many, many confessions. I re-jigged the order of the misdemeanours hoping that my confessor would not recognise me and my repeated crimes!

Rotating sins I later discovered was something many others did too. I had thought I was the only one. Back then there were so many things which were not spoken about.

Maybe, trying to 'trick' my priestly confessor was a sin in itself! I can only hope that Christ who knows all and loves the little children was on my side and forgave me.

There is one memory which I regret to say I can never forget and which re-enforces that sense of fear surrounding many aspects of Catholicism. We were practising for our First Confession when fear drove one child, the same age as me, to wet herself in the confessional. It saddens me to this day that fear was such a prominent part of religious observation. Fear of hell, purgatory or limbo. Fear of death and damnation.

Fortunately, as a child I had opportunities to focus on an upside; First Holy Communion brought rewards. I remember my godmother, Mary Byrne, who is still alive and well, giving me a 10 shilling note on the road outside our house just days before my First Holy Communion. It was a staggering amount of money and it was my first 10 shilling note. I can still see that note. My mother took it from me for safe keeping!

First Confession is still a big ordeal for children. But I sense from my own children that there is a lot less fear involved. I was also determined to ensure that they would not experience what

I had gone through. Nor would I insist that they go to confession on a weekly basis as we did.

One of my nieces when preparing for First Holy Communion asked why it was that the priest wanted to know all the bad things she did. 'Why doesn't he ask me about all the good things I do?' she implored. Why, indeed?

I went to a convent school run by the Sisters of Mercy and for the most part I have good memories of my schooldays. The Mercy nuns were, for the most part, merciful. Within their ranks there were great teachers and some very kind souls.

Confirmation was an entirely different affair. My brothers Jack and Eugene received the sacrament of confirmation at the same time as I did. I remember the suit I wore. It was a gorgeous flecked brown and tan number with a velvet collar. I wore it with a pink peaked hat, which was so fashionable at the time.

In secondary school, I cycled to Mass every day during Lent. I wore a fluffy orange hat and I can still hear and see one of my favourite teachers, a nun, now deceased, saying that there would be no peace in Ireland until such time as all women wore hats at Mass. Would that the Northern Ireland issue, later to intensify, might be so readily resolved.

We lived just outside the town of Ardee. For many years our nearest neighbours, on a seasonal basis, were traveller families. We walked to school passing their camps every day. The conditions in which they lived were shocking and disturbing. Rats ran with dogs and children ran barefoot and hungry. To my mother's great credit she tried to do something about it and with others in the town, including the nuns, actively campaigned for better living conditions for the families. At Christmas she would always cook a hot dinner and deliver it to our travelling neighbours before we ourselves sat down to eat. It was real Christianity in action, practised by a woman who was already feeding a house of 11 people. Right up to the time of her death this year (1 April 2012), the extended families of our traveller neighbours visited my mother, I presume as a sign of their regard for her and what she did in her own way to make their lives a little easier.

Religious observation loomed large in my childhood. We said the Rosary every night for years and years. My mother and father also recited the Rosary when they were together in the car. The funniest things often happened during the evening Rosary. Our dog would get up to the most embarrassing things when we prayed. My father always tried to keep a straight face but a dog misbehaving as we recited the Our Father was just too much. We would erupt into peels of laughter but order was quickly restored and the prayers continued.

Around the age of eight or nine I began to worry about death and the idea of being dead 'for ever and ever' really played on my mind. I never really told anyone about it. I would not be able to sleep and would go up to the kitchen complaining of a stomach pain. I noticed this phase in my own children and tried to help them deal with the harsh realities of this life. But finding the right words to explain away the darkness of death to a young child worrying about what would happen to his or her parents is not easy. I cannot imagine how children cope with such separation when it happens or how parents cope with the loss of children, as some inevitably have to.

As a child I silently struggled with a lot of other issues too – life issues, religion, politics and more. I think the extent to which children reflect deeply on such things is often not appreciated; they do not have the experience to express their intimate thoughts and fears.

This year we mark 50 years of RTÉ (the national broadcaster). Television was a major force for change in Irish society. In my teens *The Late Late Show*, hosted by Gay Byrne, was breaking new ground discussing issues rarely discussed in an open forum. Many of the issues were deeply uncomfortable for Irish society. At home we would always watch *The Late Late Show* on Saturday nights before we went out socialising as teenagers. We had huge debates and arguments about the issues raised and with 11 people around the table – eight children, my parents and my uncle – there was plenty of volume and many disagreements. To my parents' credit, they never attempted to stifle debate or steer it in any particular direction, they simply listened and sometimes participated. They seemed to enjoy the fact that their children – five girls and three boys – were capable of having and expressing their own opinions. I also think that they had been shackled by the rigidity of Irish society and by the rules of the church and enjoyed very much being able to witness an opening up of society.

My father was a quiet man. He loved his farming and had a very simple but deep faith. He worked every day God gave him, never complaining, other than when the weather impeded his farming routine. He took all of life's vicissitudes on the chin; the gunfire accident that left him with a limp; the burning down of our home and many other events on his life's journey. He did not speak to us very much about his faith; he just lived it well. He loved our mother and all of us and provided well for us until he died at the age of 76. A man who thought nothing of material possessions but revelled in the many interesting journeys he was able to take to an emerging Europe, to Russia, to the USA and to Canada. His most profound comment about religion was *laborare est orare* ('to labour is to pray'). He was true to his religious observations. He loved Latin hymns, hymns like *Tantum Ergo* – hymns I also love.

In 1974 I was in my first year in UCD (University College Dublin) and was heartbroken being away from home. Just as around examination time, I again found huge comfort in my faith. The church in UCD was a regular port of call for Mass and for reflection. There was a fair bit of 'religion' in my father's family. His sister Maureen is a Medical Missionaries of Mary sister now retired in Drogheda. He had a cousin who was a priest and another cousin a religious brother. When we were children they took us for long drives and outings during the summer months. We always had a great time. My aunt left home at a very young age to join Mother Mary Martin in establishing the Medical Missionaries of Mary. I am not sure how I would react today if any of my children left home so young to join a religious order.

Attending Mass on Sunday was a big part of the calendar. It was as much a social event as a religious one, when we met friends and neighbours. Inevitably some of my siblings stopped attending Mass on a regular basis, much to the sadness of my mother (my father never commented directly). I remember being worried about their prospects in the next life! Today I have a different attitude to religious observation and to how others observe theirs. My relationship with the church has evolved.

I think it is impossible – even if I wanted to – to shrug off my Catholic upbringing. There are things which are almost genetic at this stage. I like the peace experienced when attending Mass. I like and need the time it affords to reflect and slow down. Perhaps the church is the only place where I know I must turn off my mobile phone and allow my brain to slow down. I especially love to see children preparing for First Holy Communion. I love their voices, their devotion, their delight and their joy at being asked to read from the ambo and lifting the big candles. It gives me a lump in my throat, especially now as all of our four children have moved through that phase.

I have had my internal battles with the church. The role of women in the church bothers me. The scandal of child abuse upsets me deeply. My faith has sometimes been challenged but, thank God, remains strong.

Lobinstown parish in County Meath is my local church since we moved to the farm in 1997. Our parish priest, Fr Sheeren, is always worth listening to. My girls sing in the choir, guided by their now retired teacher. We are lucky to have beautiful singers. Christmas, Easter, First Holy Communion and Confirmation are always special. I wonder why it is that Catholics are so reluctant to sing out loud or join in the hymns, unlike my Church of Ireland friends.

I'm now over 50 and I can honestly say that I'm more at peace with the world.

Mass is important to me. But so too is solitude. I love walking the fields. It is where I feel closest to nature and to God and it is where I probably do most of my praying. I feel blessed that I can find such peace and comfort with myself and the world in these ordinary places, whatever the weather. My faith in Christianity has given me that. Christ was extraordinary. Great things have been done in his name, and terrible things too.

I hope my children develop a deep faith. I think they will need it to see them through the dark times and to enjoy fully the bright and wonderful days. The Catholic Church today is a very different institution from the one in which I grew up and as a living institution it will continue to change. I wonder about the future; with far fewer priests, we will all be called upon to serve in different ways. This next phase could make or break the church.

Yet despite all that has changed, parents still want to have their children baptised and receive the sacraments. They want them to belong. The fundamental principles of Christianity never change. If only we could all live by those simple, easy to understand messages, what a wonderful world it would be. Let us keep trying; it is what Christ asked of us.

A Christian Brother today

Martin Byrne

Pottering around the North Wall in Dublin where I work, or around Cherry Orchard where I live, I am constantly asked the same unsettling questions, in various terms and by different pained faces: 'Is love alive?' 'How can we stand strong as a family or as a community when the disruptive sands are constantly shifting beneath our feet to favour the well off?' 'Where is hope?' My fragile faith helps me at times to listen respectfully to these and other awkward questions and not to take short cuts in attempting an answer. The story of Jesus also helps me not to run away, but to remain anchored in kinship with pained, beautiful, desperate people, and maybe together we are better able to hear the seed of mystery growing. Sometimes, I do close off and look in a different direction. At other times, I just cannot escape the wonder.

It was Christmas Eve last year, a bitterly cold night and I had jogged into town from Cherry Orchard to sing at the Vigil Mass with the St Laurence O'Toole folk group in the North Wall. People were rushing home with the last of their shopping done. As is my habit, I called into a few homes in Sheriff Street to exchange seasonal good wishes. I had to be at the church for 6.45 p.m., as it is my job to have the microphones out for the folk-group before they sing the carols at the crib. The crib in the North Wall is special and the infant saviour is back-lit by a lantern from a Dockland's goods train. I popped my head into one home and it was a typical busy scene of many children, of final present-wrapping, of preparing for tomorrow's dinner and of getting the messages sorted away. On the kitchen table were some brown paper bags, freshly bought at the Lidl near the Five Lamps, containing chicken balls, fried rice and a variety of curry sauces. 'Sit down and join us for tea', I was invited, as the bags of food were shared out to fill and to heat all in the room. Nourished by good company, some laughs and some shared stories, as I went to leave, one of the older teenage girls asked me if I would say a prayer with the family, so that we would all be safe in the New Year. We stood in a circle, remembered and gave thanks. I am lucky to be in a place where struggling people continually bless me with good news.

Society today badly needs the recovery of a genuinely Christian gospel. There are many apparently attractive narratives placed before us by politicians and the media, but there is a dearth of hope, meaning, connectedness, respect, compassion and mystery in the air. The paralysis of much of today's church life in Ireland lies in the reality that its theology has relocated off the edges and is owned by the elite in the academy and the *ecclesia* (the church). When the voices, wisdom and cries of poor people are included in the conversation, be it in tones of humour, anger, hostility, care, compassion, resentment and confidence, then our souls are stirred and we begin to wonder. Through my life, in company with struggling people, I have been privileged to experience mystery showing itself. In the church, in social life and within my own soul I come to realise more and more that poor people have the privileged delivery system for gifting us access to the gospel. Journeying with underprivileged people, we are transformed, as mystery and humanity are revealed to us.

This mystery cloaked in a lifelong engagement, alongside people who are struggling, has been precious, and is an integral part of my story, of my soul-transformation and of my faith quest. This mystery, which we sometimes call God, has discovered and formed me in the love of my parents, through my Ballybough upbringing, in praying with the scriptures, in my desire as a young religious brother not to teach in middle-class schools, in my 14 years of enrichment in the church with people who are deaf, in working in Youthreach and in Larkin Community College and in living a simple, inserted lifestyle in the North Wall and in Cherry Orchard. Shared friendships on the street are the mutual locus of consecration. To retain a bit of sanity and health I usually jog the six miles into work daily, and annually I walk the Wicklow Way in solitude to recharge my soul. These experiences, coupled with a consciousness of my own brokenness, have constantly kept the cracks wide enough open so that the mystery can keep seeping through. In a church in Ireland that is leeching élan, or in a religious life that is moribund, such heartfelt thinking or such unusual stances are often viewed as awkward, radical, strange and unwelcome.

People on the street see me as a brother and this, in turn, is a re-construction of being a Christian Brother. Living and working in Cherry Orchard and the North Wall have helped me understand Brother through the process of being considered such by my neighbours. The people of the North Wall and Cherry Orchard gift me an understanding of my own vocation and offer me a true Christian Brother identity. In friendship, mission, engagement and immersion into the world of Dublin's Docklands I learn the deepest meaning of being brother today.

The Christian gospel in the North Wall is social at its heart and Sheriff Street theology is about the helter-skelter pilgrimage of the whole community. The process of theologising finds expression in stories, political activity, memories, poetry, song, dance, art, drama and religious rituals. The timbre can be confrontational, challenging and transformative, as much as it might be comforting, reassuring and inspirational. It is my privilege, however, to be involved at street level with the North Wall community and to be part of its turbulence, pains, joys and triumphs. With the North Wall community for the past 14 years, we have annually published a collection of stories in an urban, contextual theological style and each day I teach personal development classes in a variety of agencies within Dublin's inner city.

When the church has been heartbroken, displaced and sufficiently pummelled by the cries of poor people or by its own deep inconsistencies, it may then be humble enough to be drawn into a new way of seeing and a new way of being Christ in our world. Marinating in the silence and screams of poor people, we are opened to a new wisdom and a new name for God. Opting to live and work in the inner city as a Christian requires of me to be ready to throw away the guidebook and to walk in the dark near bog holes. In partnership with struggling people, the church can be turned around and sent to face in a new direction.

Through my Ballybough upbringing and in my years of engagement in the North Wall I have gradually experienced a shift in the locus and definition of church. Something strong in my consciousness previously viewed the church as priests, religious and respectable people in a particular place listening and responding to the cries of poor people. A residue of that consciousness that places me in a position of power and privilege remains. However, in kinship with the people of the North Wall, and especially the young adults whom I teach, I have been drawn to begin to abandon this attitude, perspective and stance. After years of gathering North Wall stories, I can state with clarity and conviction that the church is the people of the North Wall. As one among many in the community of the North Wall, it is my privilege to sit and listen to wisdom. Here among the people of the community I have been drawn to experience a new way of being church, a fresh definition of Jesus incarnate at the ordinary edges and a vibrant language for the gospel.

I value the reserves of wisdom to be found in the Catholic Church in matters of spirituality, in its social teachings, in its safeguarding of the name of Jesus, in its incarnational, sacramental focus. But most especially, I value a church that with the poor is unmasked, woken-up and burdened with the costly, glorious reality of being drawn into God's dynamic dream within history. The ghettos of Dublin's north inner city are hallowed ground and the communities there, despite many problems, continue to be a great reservoir of hope, humanity and spirituality.

Over 60 years ago I was born into a working-class family in Ballybough, in the heart of Dublin's north inner city. My soul-life is founded on the shoulders of giants: parents and ancestors who raised their families in tenements and in rural poverty. Since my childhood, I have been aware that church best takes place in all types of odd places, rituals and at all kinds of odd hours. Through life I have grown to espouse my Catholicism and a stance of prophetic, subversive orthodoxy might describe where I have positioned myself. However, being fragile and needy myself, the graces of self-doubt and of humility are regularly cultivated.

In the inner city, stories overwhelm where laughs are many, chaos swirls about and depression gives way to despair. Around the community campfire the songs of pain seldom sound like 'Alleluia'. Being a partner in birthing the new is not always a wonderful experience. The women, the grannies, the volunteers, the community leaders, the young aspiring people and many more who do their best for their families and for the community are midwives of mystery, powerful teachers and drawers to light at the edges of the abyss. I am so lucky to enjoy the friendship of Ciara who since childhood has struggled with leukaemia; Sean who after years of struggle is now involved as a leader with community education; and Brian, who as a lone parent is raising his disabled child. Around Dublin's inner city the communion of saints has very particular types of heroes.

Phyllis encourages her only child to study abroad. Marie moves her older, addicted kids out of the house for the sake of the younger ones. Jordan, whose brother was shot, brings up his daughter with no hate in her heart. Across the community, mothers often hold families and individuals together with the recession biting, when abuse issues arise in the family and when a child is sick in hospital. When security and hope are eroded, fathers and mothers fill that space with love. Granny Betty goes to England to take back her three grandchildren from social services there, and raises them as her own. Patricia with kids in jail and others strung-out, is one of my most powerful allies in the inner city.[1]

I know that I regularly get a pulse of prolonged epiphany at the Five Lamps when I am overwhelmed with the realisation that I enjoy the people of the inner city and that they hold me as a brother. In sharing stories of miscarriages, drug addictions, of heartbreak and in relishing celebrations, sing-songs and small victories, there is a vibrant unquenchable soul-force of down-to-earth love. A mutual gift-exchange of friendship and of self-giving is on offer. By the way, the inner city is not a very romantic spot, as often some kids I teach wreck their own lives, destroy their families and community and mess up other young people on the street. Each morning when I walk the streets of the North Wall and engage with the people, I have a purpose for being human, for getting out of bed and for being a Christian Brother.[2]

---

1. Biographical details and names have been altered in this essay in order to respect the anonymity of all concerned.
2. The term Christian Brother is employed here in an ambiguous fashion, standing for both my religious congregation and for a gospel lifestyle and attitude.

On the streets, as part of a struggling community, I imbibe a new name and a new face for the mystery we call God. My anesthetised heart is constantly broken. In the love and the rage of these hurting, celebratory people, I am energised to keep trying to craft a new and fairer humanity. From my friends in the inner city I gain eyes to see differently and with them I can speak a challenging truth to the privileged, with authority. These drab grey surrounds and these striking Dockland vistas are a reminder to me of the irrepressible urge to stand with these local people as they slowly free themselves. Shoulder to shoulder with these people I get hints of God stirring and of why I am pottering about these streets for the past 25 years. During all this time I have not got much done other than discovering, alongside a whole community of broken and beautiful people, that somehow this is a sacred place.

In the wake of the Ryan Report, the collapse of traditional religious life in the Western world and the buckling of the church in Ireland, we are, I believe, very well-equipped to enter into mission now as partners, with our corporate hands empty and our anguished hearts open to receive from poor people. The great richness that the Christian Brother now has to offer is not in a multiplicity of community development projects, in a model way of living in community, in professionalism or in tested templates for searching for mystery in the modern world. What we Christian Brothers have to give is our poverty and our deep scars which should better enable us to relate with poor people as brothers. In kinship and in partnership, there is both present and future mission. Poor people around the globe are waiting and willing to mentor and to gift us.

It is a bit like being one of the last of the Mohicans, staying active on the front lines as a Christian Brother in Ireland today. Around me, institutional church structures and traditional apostolic religious life are struggling for form and are not making a good fist of it, too detached from the edges and too closed-in on themselves to be vibrant and real. Dislocation, disorientation, isolation and upheavals can be, however, surprising moments of blessing. I believe I am in great company each day, working in education with a wide variety of inner city adolescents and parents, singing at Mass each Sunday with the

North Wall community and being in a position each year to publish a collection of North Wall stories. The people of the inner city ache for the divine, accentuate the human, live community and gift with life the church, of which they are an integral part. My life and my faith journey on the edges suggest a tentative, fragile, humble theology of smallness, where the gift of mystery is given to us in the most unlikely of faces and places.

The uses of Catholic guilt

Mary Kenny

As you grow older, you begin to understand that the values your elders once tried to din into your giddy head represented their valiant attempt at trying to correct human nature and Original Sin. This imbued you with 'Catholic guilt', but maybe it wasn't all negative and has its individual and social uses …

1. Catholic guilt makes you slightly nicer to people whom you don't necessarily like because you were taught that every human being has an immortal soul. This may entail, occasionally, a little hypocrisy, but then hypocrisy oils the wheels of social intercourse (except in Australia where folk tend to be dauntingly outspoken).

2. Love your neighbour, and also love your enemy, for, as G. K. Chesterton observed, they may amount to the same thing. And though you are not obliged to like everyone, you are expected, puzzlingly, to love them.

3. You'll get 3,000 days off purgatory if you visit the sick. This is an incentive to visit the sick. Or lonely.

4. Maybe twice the tariff if you visit the imprisoned, so poetically described, in the United Kingdom, as being guests of Her Majesty.

5. Your guardian angel will blush if you do something unworthy to disgrace him (he dresses like a girl, but is referred to as a boy, which might explain why Catholic countries like Brazil specialise in lavish cross-dressing).

6. When you've screwed things up – once again – your guardian angel may well remind you that you are the author of your own disasters. As, most of the time, you are.

7.   He will make you feel ashamed when yielding to *Schadenfreude* – that all-too-human malicious satisfaction in the bad luck of others, especially the ones who, until now, seemed to get all the glittering prizes.

8.   You remember your aunty Nora telling you it was wrong to cheat the transport company of its 'rightful revenue', so God will punish you if you dodge your train fare.

9.   And anyway you might get caught and that could be very socially embarrassing, like Ivor Novello found to have been cheating on his petrol rations during the Second World War.

10. The Just Man falls 77 times a day, so if you've only 'fallen' a few times, you still have a margin of error.

11. 'Mocking is catching.' God will punish you if you call in sick, and you're not really sick at all, just hung-over. So, out of guilt, you don't. Which is really a beneficial attitude to social welfare anyway.

12. 'Is sex dirty?' 'Only if it's done right.' Woody Allen's quip shows that Jewish guilt isn't so different.

13. Maybe Catholic guilt made some people feel inhibited about sex, but most of the human race seems to have managed just the same. And there are some aspects of sexuality – rape and acts of paedophilia come to mind – which jolly well should induce guilt. The porn industry isn't exactly edifying, either. Adultery causes lots of trouble in the long run. Incest makes trouble in the family. Oh yes, there are some rational causes for guilt.

14. Consider other people before yourself, and don't take the last slice of cake. At table, pass the salt to your neighbour before she has to ask for it.

15. Cleanliness is next to Godliness: although the provenance of this ideal here might well be Protestant guilt. Yet no one kept hospitals cleaner than nuns, under whose meticulous regime MRSA never broke out.

16. Give alms to the beggar, and if he's spending it on drink or drugs, that's none of your business. It could be your nearest and dearest reduced to rock bottom through life's misfortunes. If you feel guilty about giving him money, give him chocolate, which sustains.

17. Do not short-change employees. Remember that 'the sin crying out to heaven for vengeance' is 'defrauding the poor of their wages'.

18. God will punish you if you waste your gifts. Remember the parable of the talents, and the chap who buried his.

19. If you're having a bad time, offer it up. You're in a valley of tears – get used to it.

20. Through adversity, the soul is tried. Nietzsche said 'What doesn't kill me makes me stronger', and though inconveniently Nietzsche was an atheist, he picked this up from Christianity.

21. If you're too sick to go to Mass, you're too sick to go to the pictures. (Sunday prohibitions of childhood equals adult prohibitions on not treating yourself if you haven't done your duty first.)

22. You can see the point of euthanasia and mercy killing, and often it is done for compassionate reasons – but there's always that taboo that says you're just not supposed to bump people off, even with good intentions.

23. You can see the point of divorce, but as the nuns used to say, 'What would happen if everyone did it?' There would be no home life for children. So remember your mother's advice for marriage: 'Never let the sun go down on your anger, and never give a man bad news on an empty stomach.'

24. You don't agree with various popes that contraception is intrinsically evil: but there's something rather poetic and beautiful about sex representing 'the transmission of life' just the same. A bit of *Humanae Vitae* remains

lodged in the sub-conscious – maybe because nature, as much as any papal edict, put it there.

25. If you've nicked something, you must make restitution. No pardon without making amends. This idea is actually entering the criminal justice system as 'restorative justice' and about time too.

26. Judge not that ye be not judged: as sure as anything, if you fall off the straight and narrow, you'll be hoisted by your own petard.

27. Jesus Christ came on earth to save sinners, which may be why some of the non-believers you encounter are nicer people than you are, not being such sinners who have to be saved. But maybe sinners are more interesting than good people.

28. Every hair of your head is counted, so you must be a pretty unique person. DNA has come to prove what was promised in the New Testament.

29. If you particularly like a possession – give it away.

30. Be sure your sins will find you out – that bad chest condition is your punishment for 30 years of heavy smoking. Did you think you'd get away with it? Take the consequences like a brave soldier!

'We are the ones we've been waiting for': towards a poetics of hope for Catholicism in Ireland

Nóirín Ní Riain

Introduction

Nearly 2,000 years ago, Peter, fisherman, apostle and disciple of Jesus Christ, wrote a letter to his followers. He had this to say to us about how important it is to speak out our hopefulness and our desires. 'Always be ready to make your defence to anyone who demands from you an accounting for the hope that is in you' (1 Peter 3:15), he recommended.

We could be forgiven for lacking in any hope or spiritual enthusiasm for the institutional church. We could be excused for sinking into despair and anger, for jumping ship in these dry, parched deserts of post-modern, post-Celtic Tiger, post-Roman Catholic Ireland in which we live. But there is more and this is the time for it.

The current catastrophe and confusion in our church has been named as 'the worst credibility crisis in the Roman Catholic Church since the Reformation'[1] by the eminent theologian, Hans Küng. The Church of Rome, although still disgracefully inadequate in so many areas, has, to some degree, embraced the poor and the exploited. Yet, whereas we are told that 52 per cent of the world's population are women, within that same organisation they are still marginalised, oppressed, silenced and ignored. When religious institutions exclude women from hierarchies and liturgies, the inevitable subtle implication is that they are inferior. On any level of society, complete absence of the feminine – or indeed the masculine for that matter – is bound, sooner rather than later, to end in tears, tragedy and ruin. Surely if there is not justice and equality for all, then there is justice and equality for no one.

To assume that we know a person's soul, his/her deepest heart-relationship with God and his/her potential simply because of one's gender is a form of heresy. Every person's right

---

1.   See *The Irish Times*, April 2012, 'An open letter to Catholic bishops.'

to God is sacred and universal and independent of biological genitalia. The Holy Spirit herself works in many ways through every person, fully alive, as St Irenaeus (on whose feast day, 28 June, I write) says: 'The Glory of God is every person fully alive.'

The outline of this essay is as follows: firstly, I will attempt to define myself at this moment in time. Secondly, I will briefly outline my own experience as a young girl growing up in Ireland in the 1950s and 1960s, an episode which is not uncommon from others or in any way exceptional at all. Thirdly, I will relate one personal vignette of interdict and debarment without bitterness, anger or over-interpretation. It speaks for itself.

I will conclude with an appeal for a new beginning of retrieval of treasures, in scriptures, rituals and writings, which the Roman Catholic Church gifted us with, the final conclusion being that the future of Catholicism in Ireland depends on each one of us owning up, listening to our hearts, listening to each other and listening to God.

'Singing AMEN is singing your own name' – St Augustine
Amen! (So be it!) I now call myself an Irish Judeo-Christian for these reasons: Irish because, in harmony with our Celtic fore parents, I find a great reverence for and presence of the Divine in space and place. My heart imagination stirs when I am surrounded by the beauty, the godliness of landscape; *'Dia uileláithreach'* ('God ever present and all around us') as our ancestors would say. The world of natural Divinity is marvellously captured in the first poem I ever learned 'off by heart' as a young girl. Written by the journalist Joseph Mary Plunkett, also a leader of the 1916 Easter Rising, it has never become familiar or dull but is alive still, today, in every sound:

> I see his blood upon the rose
> And in the stars the glory of his eyes,
> His body gleams amid eternal snows,
> His tears fall from the skies.

> I see his face in every flower;
> The thunder and the singing of the birds
> Are but his voice – and carven by his power,
> Rocks are his written words.

All pathways by his feet are worn,
His strong heart stirs the ever beating sea,
His crown of thorns is every thorn,
His cross is every tree.

As a Christian, moreover, I am totally committed to, and love the teachings and message of Christ, the beautiful reality of the Holy Trinity and the feminine presences that weave in and out of that person of Christ. Yet all of us followers of Christ automatically draw enrichment and meaning from the ancient religious writings of Israel. Christ was a Jew, well taught and familiar with those Hebrew scriptures. He sang and prayed the psalms daily, which shaped his life and beliefs. Christ's tidings are in tune with the two great truths of the Hebrew Bible. Firstly, when the Son of God calls on 'the one who has ears to hear, listen' (Matthew 11:15), surely he is simply remembering and translating anew the great *Shema* of Israel and the first words of the prophet Isaiah: 'Hear, O heavens and listen, O earth' (Isaiah 1:2). Secondly, Christ repeats over and over the assurance that God is Creator and Saviour of the world, the ultimate Guardian Angel of all our destinies. Hence the Judeo-Christian name-tag.

Mo scéal féin – scéal gach duine (My own story, everyone's story)
Growing up in the Ireland of the 1950s and 1960s, my story and experience of Catholicism harmonises with many Irish Catholics. I was born in 1951 into a staunch Roman Catholic, County Limerick family. My mother, Nora Ryan, was the local primary school teacher and the church choir director. An attractive, independent woman, she not only gave me a great sense of prayer and ritual, but I also heard from her the first strains of Plain Chant as she taught us, choristers, to sing the marvellous Gregorian Chant chestnuts like the *Missa de Angelis – Kyrie Eleison*. Her two sisters, my Auntie Agg, a Presentation Sister, and my Auntie Mai, a St Louis Sister, were frequent visitors to our home when God-talk constantly filled our home. As a young girl keenly listening to them talking about the religious life, the liturgy, the institutional church, Vatican II reforms and so on, I was fascinated, although I was never drawn to follow

the life of the convent myself. I loved the ceremony of Sunday: dressing up in our 'Sunday best' for Mass, the family car-drive to Caherline church (the only real time I shared with two busy working parents), the sound of the Latin invitatory initial Eucharistic words – *'Introibo ad altare Dei'* – and followed by Sunday lunch, the family high-point meal-time.

My father, Paddy, was a handsome Limerick businessman. His morning ritual was to attend Mass at the Dominican church just around the corner from his office. His evening always ended kneeling at his bedside in prayer. A holy man, first action in the door of the church was to take his Rosary beads out of his pocket and for the entire Mass he went into another world of prayer as he thumbed through the beads, whispering endless Hail Marys. This practice of saying the entire Rosary daily, I inherited from him.

One of my earliest memories is of my mother bringing me to the nearby Benedictine monastery of Glenstal Abbey for the great occasion of the blessing of the new church on 26 June 1956 by Archbishop Jeremiah Kinane. I was just five years old and although it is in many ways vague, the mysterious sound of the chant still echoes gently in my heart. On that day, too, something else must have happened that I cannot articulate precisely. The connection with the sacred space of Glenstal Abbey was forged. A troubled child, lonely and introverted, I would, after that June day, frequently cycle the six-mile journey from home and feel instantly at another home here among the oak trees, the birds of the air and the swans of that front-avenue lake. The monastic residents I had yet to meet, but back then it was enough for me to steal into the back of the church when the monks gathered for vespers. Gregorian Chant then enthralled me, and still does.

A tale of two sons and a mother
I was invited, along with my two sons, to sing at a Roman Catholic European monastery. We arrived just in time for lunch, the day before the performance. We were greeted warmly by the abbot who then led us to a small room adjacent to the monastic refectory. 'This is where Nóirín dines,' he said. 'You, young

men, are coming to eat with the monks.' In shock, the lads followed, re-appearing 30 minutes later, very angry, and determined to eat with me from then on. The incredulous community reluctantly accepted.

However, when Sunday lunchtime came (the monastic culinary high-point of the week, just as we had back home in County Limerick all those years ago), we three were sitting in the women's eating area. Suddenly and out of the blue two young monks dashed in, stood behind the lads' chairs, forced them to stand insisting that they must eat with the community.

Furthermore, with great delight, one of the monks announced, brandishing two CDs immediately recognisable to us, in his right hand: 'Look, we are even having your mother singing for us in our refectory during lunch'. My sons could not resist, without causing great confusion, and off the four went, two very, very reluctantly indeed.

There I was left sitting alone listening to strains of my own voice coming from next door. I cannot put words on the deep sadness and lonesomeness that I felt then. But it was a moment of grace too, because I felt a great wave of divine presence and a warning from that same source that I wasn't to take this personally. If I did, that would be the end of my personal and spiritual growth and journey!

Postword: We are the ones we've been waiting for (Arizona Hopi Elders)
There is a truth in the tired cliché that 'we must not throw the baby out with the bathwater'. We must hold onto, revitalise so many beautiful resources from our Roman Catholic tradition. From Judaeo-Christian tradition, just open the Book of Psalms on any page and there your heart will be. Consider the ecstatic women's songs from scripture like the greatest song of salvation from the Christian tradition, the *Magnificat*. What about the mystical writings of John of the Cross, Edith Stein, Catherine of Sienna, Julian of Norwich, to name but a few, that the Catholic tradition handed down through the ages?

Moreover, I believe that rituals and liturgies from the Roman Catholic tradition must be retrieved and restored to their proper dignity in our lives. For instance, there is such a beauty in our own mantra which is the Rosary;[2] the marvellous walking meditation which is the Way of the Cross[3], or the mysteriously beautiful, haunting sound of Gregorian Chant.

The new models of Catholicism will never appear from institutionalism, clericalism, and gynecide,[4] but from each one of us, as we stand up and speak out our truths and hopes. 'Only the truth will set you free' (John 8:32), Jesus states. Every lay person[5] or perhaps a more appropriate term, every God-seeker, now has the opportunity, the obligation, to speak out and together create a magnificent community of worship and love.

I return to the Hans Küng letter of over two years ago, which although addressed to the Catholic bishops, has great accuracy and reality for every believing person. He makes six practical suggestions which I paraphrase here and comment upon: firstly, do not remain silent – in silence evil thrives. Secondly, set about reform which can only come about as a result of the first maxim. Thirdly, act together; *ní neart go cur le chéile – ar scáth a chéile a mhairimid* (In power we are together), as the ancient Irish proverbs counsel. The Arizona Hopi declaration is perfect: 'The time of the lone wolf is over. Gather yourselves!' Fourth, 'Unconditional obedience is owed to God alone … and can never be paid to any human authority: it is due to God alone.'[6] The true meaning of the word 'obedience' (two Latin words – '*ob audire*') is 'to listen intently'. Our unconditional listening and hearing is God's own possession. Fifthly, regional solutions are

2.   The Rosary is a most beautiful meditation on the life of Christ as seen through the eyes of his mother. Pope John Paul II magnified this Christian reflection when he increased the mysteries to include five 'luminous' mysteries on the life of the adult Christ. Also called the mysteries of Light, they remind us to reflect on Christ as the saving light of the world.

3.   Another marvellous form of body prayer which has a great sense of the feminine through the strong, constant presence of Mary throughout, Jesus meeting the weeping women of Jerusalem and the non-biblical presence of Veronica wiping the bruised face of Christ.

4.   This word was coined by Mark Patrick Hederman in *Underground Cathedrals* (Dublin: Columba Press, 2010), p.18. From Greek '*gyne*' which means woman and 'cide' from Latin '*caedere*' which means to kill: the 'race' to be killed or exterminated are women.

5.   This term seems to be derived from an English politics title of Lay Lord; a peer in the House of Lords other than a Law Lord. Lay person in the dictionary is described as an 'ordinary person', 'an amateur', 'non-professional', 'outsider', 'one who is inexpert!'

6.   Hans Küng, April 2012.

the answer: 'Charity begins at home.' The final call, probably the least relevant and most unlikely is that there should be a call for another Council.

As focal scoir, two sound counsels: one again from the Hopi Native American tribe: 'All that we do NOW must be done in a sacred manner and in celebration'. The other is a *Benedictus* for this new and wonderful beginning from poet and philosopher and great friend, John O'Donohue:

> This beginning has been quietly forming,
> Waiting until you were ready to emerge …
> Though your destination is not yet clear
> you can trust the promise of this opening.
> Awaken your spirit to adventure,
> Hold nothing back, learn to find ease in risk;
> Soon you will be home in a new rhythm
> For your soul senses the world that awaits you.[7]

---

7.   John O'Donohue, *Benedictus* (London: Bantam Press, 2007), p. 32.

Wrestling with Irish Catholicism

Patricia Kieran

No matter how I might critique or struggle with different notions of what it means to be Catholic, I cannot cut myself off from the Catholic faith, nor do I want to. I was born in 1962, the year that Pope John XXIII opened the Second Vatican Council that led to momentous change in the Catholic Church. I was a Vatican II baby and the product of a post-conciliar Irish Catholicism. From the 1960s onwards, younger generations across Europe exercised a greater degree of autonomy in religious attitudes and beliefs. My Catholicism bears the imprint of this cultural and historical context. While I am fundamentally a committed Catholic, I am not always conventional or conformist.

In a very direct sense my personal and professional life is firmly rooted in the Catholic faith. Catholicism has been my spiritual and academic incubator and while I'm firmly rooted in the Catholic faith, Catholicism hasn't functioned as a blinker because I'm constantly attracted by other religious and secular traditions. The little bits of travel I've done, what a friend disparagingly calls my 'spiritual tourism', to Ashrams in India, to Buddhist centres of pilgrimage or to experience the wealth of Muslim life in West Africa, have opened my body, mind, heart and soul to other spiritual pathways. The irony is that travel, and living abroad for more than 14 years, has anchored me more firmly in my own Catholic faith. I teach in a Catholic College, by profession I am a Catholic theologian and my fundamental standpoint is one which appreciates the richness of the Catholic faith, despite multiple failings in the Catholic Church past and present. As I experience it, the Catholic faith and theological tradition enable me to connect to God and others, to reverence my deepest thirst for truth, beauty, justice and mystery, in a way that nothing else can. Catholicism challenges me to live life to the best of my ability, in community, in the service of Jesus Christ and others. It challenges me but it often infuriates me.

There is so much of the Catholic tradition that I am uncomfortable with.

The older I get the more I appreciate how dynamic and changing faith is. My adult faith, as a parent, is radically different from the faith I had as a young child. Middle-aged faith is different in hue and texture from the faith of a teenager. I am acutely aware of the intersection of pre- and post-Vatican II influences in my life. My Catholic life comes in different phases. The earliest one, my infant life, was one of immersion in a Catholic *habitus* or way of being that was fairly unremarkable for rural Ireland in the 1960s. Looking back, I would say that a Catholic worldview, iconography, language and ritual impacted on almost every aspect of my family's life. All of my siblings, four girls and two boys, were given the name Mary so that my two brothers, both over six feet three inches as adults, had the name Michael Mary and James Mary on their baptismal certificates. From today's perspective there was a remarkably powerful Catholic presence in media, education, medicine, law, sport and social mores. At the time it was such a part of the oxygen that we breathed that nobody took much notice of it. I was born the youngest of seven children to John Francis Kieran and Mary Cregan. My dad, a Northern farmer from the drumlins of Louth, exiled to the lush land of County Meath, was born in 1910, and was a most devout Catholic by any standards. To my childlike mind he accepted unquestioningly everything the priest said and he encouraged his children to do the same. Obedience was a virtue. His fundamental instinct was one of acquiescence and deference to the hierarchical clerical system that was synonymous with the 'one, holy, catholic and apostolic church'. He was a loving father, a dairy farmer, who didn't seem either to struggle with or question faith. He had an extremely strong ethical sensibility, stemming from a deep sense of sin and guilt, inculcated, I suspect, by his own primary education. He was vigilant when a pencil that belonged to another child was mistakenly brought home from school by one of his children. If we kept it, this constituted theft and, armed with the weaponry of the catechism he had learned by heart in school, he cited the Ten Commandments and ensured the return of the misplaced item to its rightful owner. Fear of hell motivated him and, through his influence, us, to behave ethically. My dad was ever solicitous of the state of our souls and was fearful that his children might be in a state of mortal sin and if they died unexpectedly before receiving absolution would be consigned to eternal damnation. Every night he asked us to pray for a happy death. I couldn't see anything happy about death and, confused by the term 'to die laughing', I assumed we were praying to be asphyxiated by giggles.

Some of my generation speak of Catholicism's negative legacy on their lives, as it appeared to present everything in fearful monochrome, denying them the vibrancy of technicolour vision, leaving them wracked by scrupulosity and guilt. In my childlike world, a sense of guilt was like the News on TV, something that adults were passionate about but of little relevance to me. I knew Catholicism from the inside out, through regular spiritual practices such as going to weekly confession and Mass, the nightly Rosary, attending a mission when it visited the parish. The Catholicism of my childhood was more devotional than theologically literate or speculative but it also left an imprint on the mind and heart. At primary school I took everything literally and I had little exposure to the Bible. Nevertheless, I do remember being sad because Adam and Eve had sinned and consequently everyone in the world was denied Paradise bliss. I didn't think much of apples either after I heard that Eve's one fatal bite of the fruit denied humans perfect happiness. I wistfully contemplated that I wouldn't have to go to school, clean the house or do any work if only Eve had suppressed her appetite.

Apart from reveries like these, I was never too worried about Catholicism. Each day had a rhythmic comfort as my family said morning prayers, prayed the Angelus at midday and evening, recited the Rosary at night, and were blessed with holy water and cuddled to sleep with a kiss and a prayer at bedtime. The Sacred Heart lamp in the kitchen, the holy water font in the doorway, were the fabric and furniture of the home. Many homes around me were organised along similar lines. I knew that the sacred and the spiritual were part and parcel of every act – from saying grace before meals, to blessing the occupants of the car with holy water before embarking on a journey. These were not experienced as enforced empty rituals. They were meaningful doorways to wonder and self-transcendence.

I was a child who liked knowing where the boundaries were, but I was also interested in traversing them. The smell of incense in the church, the dim light of the Sacred Heart lamp in the kitchen, triggered an emotional and intellectual response which beckoned me beyond the immediate physical world around me. As the family said the Rosary at night, kneeling beside wooden chairs in the kitchen, I liked to look into the bright flickering flames of the kitchen fire and conjure up the terrors of eternal damnation. While hell, sin and the devil were part of my lexicon, they didn't frighten me as I experienced on a daily basis a Catholicism that was far more focused on loving God and one's neighbour. The Catholicism I experienced was neither savage nor repressive. It evoked curiosity and interest, but it was not harsh and unforgiving. Of course, my family's faith was socially reinforced by the culture and context of the time. I had no notion that anyone could view life other than the way my family did. When I was about nine or ten, I suddenly became aware that one of our neighbours belonged to the Church of Ireland and I knew that whatever that religion was, it was not Catholic. I was Catholic. To me that meant that I was ordinary. Like almost everyone I knew.

As I developed into a teenager, I could see that my parents embodied two very different types of Catholicism. My father's Catholicism was motivated by the desire to preserve official Catholic teaching and was full of absolute certainties, prescribed ritual and moral prohibitions. My mother's Catholicism was far more speculative, open-ended and critical. She was excited by a post-Conciliar Catholicism that embraced the world and recognised the need for change. She was well-educated and articulate and her mind was forever probing and questioning certainties. I remember her pondering the pettiness of the popular image of God as a divine policeman, recording human misdeeds in minute detail. She would regularly read the Bible from cover to cover and was influenced by Dag Hammarskjöld, Bede Griffiths and Teilhard de Chardin. She was hungry for democracy in the church, eager for issues of justice and gender to be taken seriously. She encouraged me to take theology seriously and felt instinctively that women's contributions to Catholicism could amount to something more than cleaning the church building, making tea at meetings or arranging flowers. While she didn't openly embody any great radicalism herself, she was always open to questioning assumptions and exploring issues from a variety of perspectives. She may not have had radical feminist desires for herself but she certainly had feminist leanings when it came to her daughters.

The fact that parents with such radically different outlooks could both be legitimately at home in the Catholic Church gave me a glimpse of a Catholicism that was broad and inclusive. I love the notion of Catholicism that acknowledges that the Catholic Church is a global phenomenon, embracing myriads of cultures and languages, in both the northern and southern hemispheres, a place where old and young, radical and conservative, devotionally pious and irregular practitioners, theological erudite and neophyte, belong.

When I was 16, my dad died suddenly from heart failure. Experiencing death first-hand as an adolescent led me straight to ultimate questions and meaning. I was nagged by doubt and uncertainty. The more I asked questions about the Catholic faith, the more dissatisfied I became with the answers that were given to me. Like most adolescents, I wanted to know about life, death and everything in-between and I was drawn to theology as a discipline that could enable me to search for meaning. I had no notion that there were different schools of theology within Catholicism or different Christian denominations doing theology from different perspectives. I just wanted to set out on the adventure of asking questions about God and seeing if the answers given to me made any sense. I was lucky that my mother was fully supportive of the venture and that I had a very positive first-hand experience of Catholicism. I went to boarding school with the Mercy Sisters in Trim. They were a fine, caring, generous community of sisters who welcomed their boarders into the convent as if we were at the pre-entry stage to religious life. This was a no frills and no nonsense school in the spirit of Catherine McAuley that gave us a good grounding in the basics of the curriculum and a sense of social justice. Nothing fancy. Nothing extra. Each day we prayed the divine office, nightly

Rosary, and celebrated daily Mass with the Sisters. I was no mystic but, while I might have moaned about it at the time, in some way I actually liked the routine and comfort of the convent life, with the shimmering candles in the early morning light or the smell of incense at Benediction in the evening. It was safe. We were largely a happy group of children living with the Sisters. We were also steeped in their spiritual practices. It was great to escape home at the weekends to non-cloistered life, but life in the convent gave us a surprisingly rich spiritual and ethical diet.

After the Leaving Certificate, I decided to study theology and religious education at the Mater Dei Institute, Dublin – the only place where lay women were able to study Catholic theology at the time. As far as I'm concerned, my study of theology illustrates that diversity of opinion and practice is part of the pulse of Catholic life. There are multiple perspectives and interpretations on all theological issues. Of course there is frequent contestation over what is orthodox and what is heterodox and the Catholic Church has mechanisms for deciding and promulgating orthodox teaching. However, the Catholic faith that I am at home with is one which respects diversity of opinion, freedom of conscience and is broad enough to provide a home for a cacophony of voices, some orthodox, some radical. The fact that the church has official teaching, presented for instance in the *Catechism of the Catholic Church*, does not mean that church members simply have to replicate this thinking and abdicate responsibility for developing and critiquing doctrine.

I've been privileged to have been able to study with brilliant Catholic theologians who are dynamic, critical, funny, creative women and men. I travelled to London and Paris to do my master's and doctorate in theology. My own doctoral research was heavily influenced by John Henry Newman's work on the development of doctrine. As a convert, Newman appreciated that Catholicism is not static and fossilised. It is dynamic and open to change. However, he presented criteria to evaluate legitimate change within the Catholic Church. Newman's notion of change might frighten people who want things to remain the same forever. Like Miss Haversham, some people don't want to change a single ornament in their intellectual and spiritual house. For me, change or diversity within the church is not a sign of weakness or error. I certainly experienced diversity in my home at a microcosmic level in the debates stimulated by two committed Catholic parents with very different views. I began to see from an early age that debate, disagreement and heterogeneity are facts of life in the Catholic tradition and a vibrant church is a church where these flourish.

In my late teens, belonging to the Catholic Church was like walking around in uncomfortable, ill-fitting, second-hand clothes. I hadn't chosen this faith tradition for myself. It was my parents' faith more than my own personal commitment that kept me attached to the church. I was a hybrid cultural and conviction Catholic. I was also fascinated by atheism and decided to do my master's thesis on the topic. I saw theology as a means of asking questions and searching for answers that would make sense to me. Anslem's classic definition of theology is 'faith seeking understanding'. For me it was more a question of understanding seeking faith.

In my 30s and 40s I began to realise that while I could play with the language of faith in a detached academic game, it was ultimately meaningless if that faith wasn't personal to me. The most profound religious experiences of my life took place in the cathedral of life. They were not engineered or foreseen. They resulted from my dad's death, falling in love, the birth of my five children and the death of friends. Through these events the words of the familiar Catholic doctrines or prayers that I'd unthinkingly rattled off were impregnated anew with divine significance. They connected me with God the Creator, Father, Son and Spirit, in a way that nothing else had ever done. I learned, from the heart outwards, through the wisdom of the body and the mind, that ultimately I was not in control of birth, life or death. These were experienced as gifts, given through me and to me, or as presences snatched from me, that opened me into ever-widening circles of divine mystery.

Catholic theology is sometimes dismissed as abstract, uncritical and irrelevant. I experienced it as an intellectually rigorous and challenging discipline. Theology helped me to begin to think about my own faith and the faith of others in a way that was not divorced from life. I am not a Catholic because of any one abstract theological formula, but theology has certainly helped me to think through my struggling faith and to learn from others, including those of no faith or those of different faiths. I love the biblical story where Jacob wrestles with God (Genesis 32) and his name is changed to 'Israel', meaning one who struggles with God. I can identify completely with being a person of Israel, of often being jostled by questions which lead to uncertainty and a further search for, and openness to, God.

Catholicism comes from the Greek phrase *kath'holou*, meaning 'according to the whole', and has connotations of universality. I believe that the Catholic religious family should be characterised by inclusivity and welcome. Yet the ideals presented in the gospel values of Jesus Christ, the love which touches the lepers, speaks to the culturally shunned Samaritan woman, celebrates the giftedness of children, joyfully awaits the coming of the kingdom of justice and peace, are often blatantly at odds with the incomplete and broken faith life experienced by many members of the Catholic Church. Hans Küng speaks of the *'un-church'*, the underbelly of the church, which is evident in shameful activities such as Islam phobia, misogyny, inactivity in the face of injustice, apathy in the face of global and environmental disaster, the abuse of power, indeed wherever the church fails to live up to the gospel values and its own teaching. The *'un-church'* occurs where great injustice is perpetrated in the name of the church.

The Catholic Church is far from perfect. One need only mention the Ferns, Ryan, Murphy and Cloyne Reports for Catholics to hang their heads in shame. The treatment of children within the church and a host of other painful issues highlight the chasm between the actual and the possible. In the face of a growing secular Irish society, there is open and public disenchantment with the Catholic Church. I too am critical of the church. I am also sceptical of a form of official Catholicism that engages in a theological frisking of its members to scrutinise their stance on key issues (usually homosexuality, married clergy, ordained ministry for women, divorce) and which censures or silences them if their answers do not conform to official church teaching and they are prominent members of the academy or society.

My own study of the history of Catholic theology shows me that contemporary crises within Irish Catholicism, painful and serious as they are, must be placed in the context of an evolving faith tradition that spans millennia and that changes at an incredibly slow pace. I am also acutely aware that God the Father, Son and Spirit, the sacred scriptures, and the rich bedrock of Catholic tradition and Magisterium are central to the Catholic faith and not, as some might think, the Magisterium of the church alone. I also know that my perspective is partial, incomplete and subject to bias. As a Catholic, I am glad to be part of the worldwide Catholic Church and while I may be overwhelmed by events that occur in Ireland, acquaintance with the issues and concerns of Catholics elsewhere in the northern and southern hemispheres puts the Irish Church into wider global context. I am open to the promptings and the work of the Spirit in the Catholic faith community and beyond. I experience Catholicism as flawed, yet I try to look deeper than the immediate or local or contemporary. I love the Mass refrain where the community collectively states that 'we wait in joyful hope for the coming of our Saviour Jesus Christ'. I want to wait with a community that is joyfully hopeful and that has reason to hope.

As an educator I am constantly heartened by my students who are open-minded, interested and curious about theology and spirituality. I am excited by a Catholicism that never gives up searching and that makes connections between the Christian faith tradition and every part of human experience. I know many members of the Catholic faith in Ireland and elsewhere who inspire me and who help to counterbalance the limitations of the Catholic Church. This is not to say that I don't take recent scandals and failures seriously. However, I don't want to become overwhelmed by them. I want that negative energy, that sense of shame, to propel me into being part of a church that tries more adequately to respond to the vision of Jesus Christ. As a parent of young children, I know it's inadequate to exclusively blame the hierarchy, the Vatican or the media for the multiple limitations of Catholicism and contemporary culture. I need to start taking a look at myself and at my responsibility to my local and worldwide church and community. Blaming others for all the limitations of Catholicism can conveniently let me off the hook. I need to grow up in my faith and to stand up for my faith. I need to put it into practice if it is to mean anything for my children, for my students and, ultimately, for me.

The faith to change

Patrick Claffey

Abandoning certainties

Dom Charles Foucher, the late prior of the monastery of Notre Dame de Kokoubou, was one of those people one meets and never really forgets. I first met him in 1986 when I went to start a parish in a rural area in the north of the Republic of Benin, West Africa, where he and a small group of four Cistercian monks from the Abbaye of Bellefontaine in France had established a monastery some 25 years previously in a remote area of 'the bush'. I came to know him very well over the following years as I visited him regularly, often on a Sunday afternoon when he was more than happy to take a break from Trappist silence to talk and have a tepid bottle of the dreadful *Beninoise* beer.

Charles by his own definition was a Vendéen peasant, with all that this implies: Catholic, French (in that order), *républicain*, but perhaps with some reservations, unapologetically right of centre in his politics to the extent that he never discussed them, and forthright in expressing his often strongly held views. He was a Trappist to the depths of his being. He found it amazing that Irish Cistercians demurred at the use of this term to indicate the followers of St Bernard of Clairvaux, to the point, he claimed, where at one time they apparently threatened to leave the Order rather than be known as Trappists.[1] Charles had no such qualms; for him *l'Abbé de Rancé*[2] was the great reformer of the Order and the monastery at Kokoubou was very much a reflection of that. The monks led a life of intense prayer and great simplicity, even austerity, living from their own work, producing their own food and supporting the monastery through the

---

1.   Thomas Merton has pointed out that the Irish Cistercians of the Strict Observance deemed the reforms of the Abbé de Rancé at La Grande Trappe in the eighteenth century to have moved beyond being 'strict' to being excessively harsh.
2.   Abbot and reformer of Notre Dame de la Trappe (1626–1700). See http://www.latrappe.fr/article3. Accessed 30 June 2012. See also Thomas Merton, *The Waters of Siloe* (New York: Houghton Mifflin Harcourt, 1979).

usual monastic sales of jams, honey, yoghurt and other produce
– *ora et labora* in a very pure form. Having read Thomas Merton
quite extensively when I was younger, I found much that was
attractive here, without ever harbouring even the slightest
illusion that I could live a Trappist life. It was, however, a life
that questioned me in its authenticity and indeed questioned
the world in its radical commitment. The monks were all clearly
men with an intense interiority, detached in one sense but at the
same time hugely interested in the world and everything that
was going on. Recently it was as if I had met them again when I
saw the marvellous Xavier Beauvois film *Des hommes et des dieux*
(*Of Gods and Men*, 2010), which tells the story of the monks of
Tiberine, Algeria who lived and died in that obscure monastery.

We became good friends over the following years and I
spent a lot of time in conversation with Charles, sometimes
when faced with difficult situations but more often in general
terms relating to faith, the church and the world we lived in.
While by his own admission he was not a theologian in the
academic sense, Charles had been 'doing theology' for almost 50
years. He was deeply versed in the Christian scriptures, the
Fathers of the Church, the Rule of St Benedict and, of course, the
writings of Bernard of Clairvaux. More important than the
simple reading of these texts, which he did for several hours
every day, was the fact that he had spent a lifetime reflecting on
them and making them his own. They had fashioned him
and made him the person he was: self-assured, forthright,
sometimes even gruff, but with the kind of faith that is surely
imperishable. He had little time for cheap pieties and his acid
test in discerning the vocation of a novice was based as much on
his willingness to take up the hoe and work the land as it was on
the time he wanted to spend on his knees in prayer. Sentimental
devotionalism in the spiritual life was clearly something he
viewed with a great degree of circumspection, not to say
outright scepticism, saying that it simply would not stand the
vicissitudes of life and human frailty. *Ora* of course, but don't
forget the *labora* and ultimately the two should be one:[3] there
was, in fact, a oneness in his life that I have only rarely met.

3.　　The essential spirit of the Rule of St Benedict is expressed in the motto *pax*
　　　and the traditional *ora et labora* (pray and work).

One of the most memorable stories Charles told me in those years was that of Dom Jean-Marie Chouteau (1841–1929), who had been elected Abbot of Bellefontaine at the exceptionally young age of 25. He remained in charge of this large monastery for the following 63 years, largely shaping it not just in terms of its physical structure but also its spirit.[4] In the days before his death, Dom Jean-Marie was brought to the infirmary in the monastery for the first time in his life, where the brother in charge asked him if he thought perhaps he should call a doctor. His response was a perfect example of a Cistercian economy of words but also a reflection of his profound faith: 'I never needed a doctor to live; I don't need one to die.' Three days later Jean-Marie Chouteau quietly slipped away to meet his Maker.

The story was surely a reflection on Charles' own faith and the basis on which he had built his life. In what was perhaps the closest he ever came to speaking with me of his personal *credo*, he once said to me: 'Patrick, I could live without 75 per cent of my certainties.' Significantly perhaps, he did not elaborate on which of his certainties he could so easily abandon and which he would tenaciously cling to but one had the distinct impression that dogma did not play a big part in the latter category. Like all the great spiritual traditions, Christian and others, this kind of ascetic life, lived for that long, will surely either make or break a man. It will lead him to distil the essence of what he believes and it leaves little place for theological mind games, false certainties or anything other than the essential truth about God and about the 'self'. Charles Foucher, who died some years ago, would probably have been too modest to claim he had absolute knowledge of God or greater self-awareness than any other person but it was without doubt the path he followed during his 50 years of Trappist life.

The idea for this essay came to me while I was travelling in India on what I saw as a kind of 'pilgrimage' in this land of a thousand pilgrimages. I was, I suppose, one of what Rowan Williams has described as 'a whole generation of new pilgrims … wishing to cut through the clutter of institutions, and achieve

---

4. See http://www.bellefontaine-abbaye.com/abbaye/histo.htm. Accessed 30 June 2012.

self-discovery in a new place'.[5] For many of my generation, India, with its rich heritage of spiritual traditions, has long been a favoured destination. Something there seems to have captured our imagination and our sense of searching. It is unquestionably a place in which to be challenged and to gain a very different perspective on the world. I have for many years been an admirer of the great British journalist Mark Tully, whose critical but sympathetic reports from India on the BBC World Service initially sparked my interest in the sub-continent. His more recent BBC radio programme, *Something Understood*, was a marvellous investigation of a rich variety of themes – human, spiritual and religious – which very much reflected the influence of India on his thinking in its openness and the search for what is true. In one of his recent books Tully places great emphasis on 'the experience of God' but also on 'the uncertainty of certainty' in terms my friend Dom Charles would surely have recognised.[6] Like him, Tully shies away from dogmatic certainties, theological or secular. Looking to the East for another kind of 'enlightenment', he quotes R. C. Zaehner, former Professor of Eastern Religion and Ethics at Oxford, who asserts that Hinduism retains its relevance, strength and vitality because unlike the Semitic religions it does not feel the need to think in dogmatic terms:

> Hindus do not think of religious truth in dogmatic terms: dogmas cannot be eternal but only the transitory, distorting images of a truth that transcends not only them, but all verbal definition. For the passion for dogmatic certainty that has racked the religions of Semitic origin, from Judaism itself, through Christianity and Islam to the Marxism of our day, they feel nothing but shocked incomprehension.[7]

5.   Cited by Robert MacFarlane, 'The road more travelled', in *The Guardian*, 16 June 2012, Review, p. 20.
6.   Mark Tully, *India's Unending Journey* (London: Rider, 2007), p. 41.
7.   R. C. Zaehner, *Hinduism* (Oxford: OUP, 1982), cited in Tully, *India's Unending Journey*, p. 9. See also Wendy Doniger, *The Hindus: An Alternative History* (New Delhi: Penguin, 2011).

The magisterial and the maternal

Sadly, for the past several decades my church (and I use the possessive pronoun advisedly) has often seemed to be obsessed with a desire for dogmatic certainty and doctrinal conformity. Still ill at ease with modernity and seemingly in retreat from its encounter with the world following the Second Vatican Council, it has sought to reassert itself through the often punitive suppression of theological reflection and debate in favour of magisterial pronouncements and the arid restorationism shown in the recent liturgical reforms and the general tenor of statements and declarations from the Vatican, including the recent summary of the *Findings of the Apostolic Visitation* following the investigation into the Church in Ireland. John XXIII spoke of the church as *Mater et Magistra*.[8] It is unfortunate, but perhaps not surprising in such a male-dominated institution, that the magisterial has so often come to take precedence over the maternal. We have lost the pilgrim sense of being 'the people of God' searching for truth in favour of a theological and spiritual elitism that at its worst can seem sectarian.

So like many Catholics today my relationship with my Church is an uneasy one. I refuse to give it up since it is where I was born and where I intend to remain. It is where I find light and truth, most often in the witness of the people, the ordinary Christians I meet. However, I am one of many in my own generation who have come to find it an increasingly cold place, often even sectarian in its intolerance of dissenting views and out of touch with where many Catholics are at in their spiritual lives. The *sensus fidelium* has been largely ignored on a whole range of questions where the faithful are in fact best qualified to speak, Also, a single theological view has become dominant, a view that is marked by a suspicion of the world and a fear of any change that might be perceived as a 'rupture' with the past or real theological questioning. In an essay on Joseph Ratzinger's approach to liberation theology, James Corkery writes about his 'attitudinal disposition toward things [theological] that contain elements he dislikes'.[9] Corkery points to his strong tendency to

---

8.   Pope John XXIII, *Mater et Magistra*, Rome, 1961.
9.   See James Corkery, *Joseph Ratzinger's Theological Idea: Wise Cautions and Legitimate Hopes* (Dublin: Dominican Publications, 2009), Chapter 9.

go for their jugular rather than, in a more discerning patience that allows the wheat and weeds to grow together, to sift them in due time. The list of theologians who have faced the grim face of the Congregation for the Doctrine of the Faith (CDF), for an examination of 'certain aspects' of their theology, is long and varied, going back to the early liberation theologians (Gustavo Gutiérrez and Leonardo Boff, amongst others) to the Belgian Jesuit Jacques Dupuis for his work on religious pluralism, and perhaps most often that of moral theology in what seems like an obsession to 'weed out' any signs of questioning which is often characterised as 'dissent'. There is indeed a real sense of fear amongst researchers and intellectuals within the church. Again certain aspects of the recent visitation reports were a clear indication of this.[10] But the church in Ireland, as well as elsewhere, needs so much more than this.

Irish Catholicism, a 'scène de crise'

It is almost impossible to overstate what has become of the church following the avalanche of revelations of institutional and sexual abuse over the past two decades. What we have witnessed in Irish Catholicism is the catastrophic implosion of what was thought by many to be an untouchable institution. Despite attempts to paper over the cracks and to present a united front in public, the hierarchy appears to be increasingly divided in itself, something that was previously unthinkable – at least in public – and alienated not just from the faithful but from an increasingly large number of the remaining priests. For many critics of the church, it now looks more like the welcome demise of a virtual theocracy. For others, the situation has many of the marks of a biblical exile. 'Exile' is certainly not too strong a word and it may, in the end, not even adequately describe what has happened. Speaking in equally scriptural terms but with a more apocalyptic tone, one female churchgoer described what has happened as a tsunami. Many of the victims of abuse, quite understandably, have spoken of it in terms of a 'holocaust'. All of these terms seek to express the unspeakable horror of what has happened to us, as a church and as a people. It is our

---

10.   See Patrick Claffey, 'Rome's wider remit', *The Tablet*, 21 March 2011, http:
      //www.thetablet.co.uk/article/16018.

darkest hour – and it is far from over. It is certainly what Michel de Certeau, writing of seventeenth-century France, described as a *scène de crise*, a moment of rupture or a paradigm shift from one socio-cultural reality to another, when the weight of socio-political and indeed moral authority shifted definitively from one institution to another, essentially from the religious institution to the modern state, and this at a time when the state itself is struggling to maintain its credibility and has seen its sovereignty all but ceded to international economic and political institutions.[11] As Michael Cronin points out, we live in a time where we have 'inherited new states of fear that are profoundly dehumanising and destructive in their consequences'.[12] It is, he argues, a time when 'hope matters'.

Finding hope
The question is: Where is hope to be found? It is certainly not to be found in magisterial chiding, in a return to an illusory 'Golden Age', or in the restoration of theologies and models that have failed. While the church in Ireland is certainly in a deep crisis, faith has not disappeared. It is still to be found in the lives of people and in the lives of many communities around the country. However, it often lies untapped, private and largely passive. Archbishop Martin caused some controversy in 2010 when he called for the bar of Catholic lay intellectual debate in modern Ireland to be raised if Irish Catholics are to effectively confront the crisis in the Irish Church.[13] The reality, of course, is that this kind of debate has been consistently stifled and there is little sign of any willingness to engage with it now as the recent visitation and summary reports indicate. A process of truncated listening where the answers have already been formulated

---

11. See Albert Bastenier, 'Le croire et le cru: Les appartenances religieuses au sein du christianisme européen revisitées à partir des travaux de Michel de Certeau', in *Social Compass*, 54 (1), March 2007, pp. 21–2.
12. Michael Cronin, 'Fear and Loathing in the Republic: Why Hope Matters', in P. Claffey, J. Egan, and M. Keenan (eds), *Broken Faith: Why Faith Matters*. This book of essays, drawn from a conference held in Milltown Institute in 2010, is currently being prepared for publication.
13. See Diarmuid Martin, 'John Henry Newman – Faith and Reason: The Ireland of Newman and the Ireland of Today'. Address given at 'Popoli' meeting, Rimini, 24 August 2010.

serves little purpose when what is required is a much broader and more open process, coming out of scripture and tradition, but with a genuine openness to the world. The 1850 Synod of Thurles was surely one of the decisive events in the history of Irish Catholicism, as it sought a root and branch reform of the Irish Church, albeit with a view to making it more Roman. A similar event should surely be envisaged at this point, even if its results are to be very different. It is surely time to free up the *sensus fidelium* and to go to where the energy is in the church and to where the Spirit is moving. It is simply not enough to dismiss such an event as a 'talking shop' or to be fettered by the fear of change. Let us have the courage to follow the advice of the poet Rabindranath Tagore: 'Let go of what must go!/it will cause you hurt/if you do not open the door/to let it out.'[14] If we do take the risk, we will no doubt be surprised at how much survives and how much binds us together as a church in the world.

---

14.   Rabindranath Tagore, *A Taste of Tagore: Poetry, Prose, Prayers* (Devon: Green Books, 2011), p. 146.

Over the garden hedge: a Church of Ireland gaze at Roman Catholicism today

Richard Clarke

To use the language of a love–hate relationship would certainly be vulgar hyperbole, but I suppose I might reasonably describe my relationship with Roman Catholicism as one that is both joyful and problematic. Hence the logical place for me to begin an essay of this nature is probably with my own understanding of my ecclesiological relationship with the Roman Catholic tradition of the church. It is certainly not a perception that accords with official Roman Catholic teaching on the matter and this, perhaps, is part of the problem.

I regard myself as being a priest and bishop of the church of God, called to episcopal ministry in a diocese (Meath and Kildare) and thus in an ecclesiastical province (the Dublin or 'southern' province of the Church of Ireland) within the Western tradition of the church universal, although sadly not in full communion with the Roman Catholic Church, nor with the Orthodox churches of the Eastern traditions of Christianity. I therefore see the Roman Catholic Church not wholly as 'other', but simply as a different tradition within that fuller church in which I express a complete belief each time I say the Nicene Creed – 'One, holy, catholic and apostolic'. Aspects of the Roman Catholic tradition may irritate me, but then aspects of my own tradition within the church also aggravate me, and at times to a far greater extent.

Henry McAdoo, a former Archbishop of Dublin and one of the doyens of the modern ecumenical movement in his chairmanship of the first meetings of the Anglican–Roman Catholic International Commission, was given to languid, if somewhat haughty, epigrams. One such was: 'I like to think that if I hadn't been born an Anglican I would have become one.' I might not choose to express the matter in quite such a self-assured manner, but I too am an Anglican from utter conviction. I believe that Anglicanism retains a full catholicity, that it achieves a reasonable if at times uneasy balance between individual conscience and responsibility on the one hand and, on the other, the authority of the church as derived from the definitive witness of the scriptures, the tradition of the church through Christian history, and the place of human reason. It also orders its life in a manner that maintains Catholic episcopal authority, but in the setting of the comprehensive participation and involvement of the whole people of God in the life of the church. (Such an ecclesiology is, incidentally, not merely a modern invention of convenience and I would argue that such a model of church is not far removed, in particular, from the teachings of one of the greatest of the third century Church Fathers, Cyprian of Carthage, but this is another matter.)

Having explained why I am an Anglican, I should point out that the lack of a clear central Magisterium, accompanied by a somewhat inchoate relational structure between its culturally diverse provinces, does make Anglicanism distinctly untidy, inexact and messy, and hence often exasperating to those of us who are part of it and, even more certainly, to those who are not. But then, I am not convinced that any tradition can be entirely faithful to Christ if it is obsessively neat and compulsively over-tidy. Even Saint Paul, not the least confident of individuals, could confess to the Corinthians that he was encountering the truth and glory of God only 'through a glass, darkly' (1 Corinthians 13:12).

Although from the Roman Catholic perspective my ecclesiastical status would technically be that of a baptised layperson in a sect that had broken away from the true church, this happily does not appear to be the understanding *de facto* of most of my Roman Catholic friends (ordained and lay), almost all of whom seem to regard me as a priest and bishop of the church, albeit not of their own tradition. It has in fact been the friendship of many individuals that has brought me to love a great deal of what the Roman Catholic Church is. In brief, I have been enabled to understand in the heart as much as in the head how my vision of Catholicity needs the presence of Christian traditions other than my own to make 'my' Catholicism a spiritual reality. I would always and readily have given intellectual assent to the precept that the Anglican tradition does not (and cannot) encompass the entirety of Catholicism (and indeed no serious Anglican writer has ever suggested otherwise). But an ever-deepening engagement with the lived faith of Roman Catholic friends has enforced the belief that true Catholicism is larger, greater and deeper than any one tradition. In recent times, I have become involved in Anglican–Orthodox theological dialogue at international level and this participation in the life of the Orthodox churches has unsurprisingly strengthened my sense of the glorious immensity of Catholicism, properly understood. Inevitably my major engagement on a day-to-day basis has been with the largest of the western traditions of the Church Catholic, the Roman Catholic Church. It is a relationship that I have come to value hugely.

My participation in the life of the Order of Preachers (principally here in Ireland but also in Rome) and in the Community of Sant' Egidio in the eternal city itself, has been an enormous strength and encouragement to me, both personally, and as a bishop and priest in ministry. Not only have I received loyal friendship and generous hospitality in abundance from both Sant' Egidio and the Dominicans, but I have also learned much from each that has strengthened my own discipleship, in times of weakness as in times of strength. 'Only connect!' has long been a favourite dictum of mine, purloined – albeit normally out of context – from E.M. Forster's *Howard's End*. The larger context of this phrase from Forster is of some value, as the paragraph continues: 'Only connect the prose and the passion, and both will be exalted, and human love will be seen at its height.' In their very distinctive ways, it seems to me that the Dominicans and the Sant' Egidio Community each connect the prose and the passion. The Dominicans do this by linking seamlessly the intellectual and reasoned aspects of gospel proclamation with a community life of discipline, prayer and generosity; the Community of Sant' Egidio makes the vital connection of coalescing communal prayer with service of the poor as a single integrated activity rather than as two. The Order of Preachers and the Community of Sant' Egidio are by no means unique in what they do but – for this Christian pilgrim – they have been a particular light on the pathway of discipleship, and have provided a powerful and moving awareness in my life of what the Roman Catholic tradition can and does give to the world.

This is not to suggest that other communities and religious orders, including some within the Anglican family, do not also accomplish truly wonderful work for God and humankind (and even in the same areas) but, for me at least, there is something of the strong sense of both *focus* and *grace* in the gospel 'being done' by both of these particular communities that has truly energised me in my discipleship, and for which I am intensely indebted to the Roman Catholic tradition as a whole.

There are a number of reasons – scarcely surprisingly – why I would find it difficult ever to become a Roman Catholic. Paradoxically, they are intimately connected with reasons why I would also find it impossible to live fully without this particular tradition of the church somewhere in my life. I would certainly find it extremely problematic to accept any ecclesiology that centralises ecclesial authority to the degree that is apparent in present-day Vatican polity – ultimately, indeed, to a single human individual, the Pope. I find myself puzzled by the apparent need to portray at all costs – and there is most certainly a real moral cost – a purportedly monolithic and unblemished image *qua* institution to the world (which is of course not even remotely duped by the attempt). And I am both distressed and offended by the institutional *de jure* belittling of other Catholic traditions – including Anglicanism – to a status of 'ecclesial communities', the clear intention being to connote an assemblage which is insufficiently similar to Roman Catholicism to warrant the dignity of church.

Having said all this (and said it somewhat brusquely), I would then have to confess that this very solidity, firmness and massive sense of self-confidence and innate security are all elements that I need to know are to be found within the totality of Catholic Christianity, even if I could not fit easily within this particular schema. In short and with no condescension whatsoever (whatever for the inherent paradox), I need to have Roman Catholicism there for me in all its beauty, strength and self-assurance, even if I do not believe that I could ever become a Roman Catholic. This theme may however require more exploration, for it suggests a more general *leitmotif* of symbiosis.

'Symbiosis' is the technical term – as much scientific as theological – which describes the relationship between two organisms that are quite distinct, but which each require the existence of the other in order that both may flourish, but without a fusion of the two. This is far more than a mere balancing of different forces in order to achieve equilibrium. Rather it suggests dynamism, vitality and creativity. My belief is that just as within Anglicanism, a strong Catholic emphasis in some quarters requires the symbiotic existence of a dynamic evangelicalism in other quarters of church life (and vice versa) in order for both to flourish in a wholesome way for the common good, Roman Catholicism and Anglicanism may in the same way need one another for the good of both. (This is not to suggest that the full ecumenical project must not be pursued with continuing and increasing energy and imagination, merely that a new relationship should be forged that will respect the values and contributions of each to the life of the other.) A faintly satirical analogy may assist in the explication of what I would want to suggest.

At present – intentionally eschewing, in order to avoid distraction, the language of 'sisters', 'mothers and daughters' or even 'fathers and (possibly prodigal) sons' – there is a relational culture between Roman Catholicism and Anglicanism that parallels a not entirely satisfactory family. And so, for our purposes, a young nephew represents Anglicanism and an old uncle represents Roman Catholicism. The uncle regards the nephew as essentially likeable, but utterly irresponsible, confused and incautious; a well-meaning young man who is nevertheless damaging the family name (and endangering the family legacies) by his insistence on constantly speaking his mind without careful thought (and on matters about which he knows precious little), by flying kites that should remain firmly grounded, and by conducting some clearly mad experiments that may explode in his face and cause collateral damage to others, including the uncle. At times the uncle is even disinclined to admit his family relationship with the nephew, implying that he might not actually be his 'real' nephew. Turning to the nephew, he still rather likes his old uncle and certainly recognises and respects his place of seniority within the family circle. However, he does not much like his uncle's constantly disapproving attitude and his insistence that the family name and reputation are more important than being transparent about the realities of family life. He knows that his uncle is kind, but he also wishes that his uncle would accept that one may sometimes have to make mistakes, to admit to confusion, and to try risky new things, without worrying about what the neighbours would say, or whether or not one might appear muddled. He is also deeply hurt by his uncle's aversion to regarding him as a 'real' member of the family, as though his parentage was suspect.

Such an evaluation of the two Christian traditions may seem somewhat cruel and even unfair, but I firmly believe that it contains enough of the truth not to be wholly parody. This truth is that our uncle and nephew do really need each other, not to mould the other into their own individual image and likeness, but instead to bring out the very best in the other, and so in themselves also. The nephew needs the uncle's traditional common sense, solidity and broader sense of priorities. The uncle needs the willingness of the nephew to admit to confusion and muddle in the interests of finally getting things right or at least making them better. They need to respect each other fully and, more particularly, they need truly to love each other.

Almost all the Christian traditions on this island have had to re-focus their sense of mission, as they come to terms with the realities of a cultural secularism that seems, very swiftly and disconcertingly, to have engendered populist support for a more widespread secularisation of Irish society. This is not of itself a catastrophe for the church or for any of its traditions. For too long we have assumed, and taken as our birthright, a place at the top table of Irish life. In a new context and also, I would hope, with a deeper and ever-deepening respect for what the other Christian traditions have to offer to the life of the whole Church Catholic, a new and lowlier place in Irish society may in fact bring the renewal of all the people of God, of whatever tradition, to a greater wholeness and holiness. To leave the last words with a poet – John Donne – who knew both the Roman Catholic and Anglican traditions from within, and who lived in far more dangerous and treacherous times than we may ever know: 'Humiliation is the beginning of sanctification.' And this we assuredly both need.

From Bansha to Mountjoy: and back again ...

John Lonergan

When I was born in 1947, the Catholic Church had a very strong influence and, dare I say, a firm grip on life in Ireland, and in particular in rural Ireland. I was the third in a family of eight children and my first awareness of the Catholic Church was when my younger brothers and sisters were christened. We lived in the country, about one mile from Kilmoyler church in County Tipperary, which stands on its own in the open countryside. In those days babies were christened within a week or so of birth and back then christenings were relatively simple family events, nothing like as big as they are nowadays. After the religious formalities at the church, usually held after Sunday Mass, there would be a small celebration in the family home – indeed, calling it a celebration might even be a bit strong. It really only involved a meal with the immediate family and the godparents, with a few bottles of stout for the men and a glass of sherry or a mineral for the women. As a small child I was so excited to get a cup of red lemonade and that was certainly the highlight of our christenings as far as I was concerned. Anyway, from the religious side of things we were told that the baby was christened when the priest poured water over its head and then the baby was given a name and that was it. Two local people, a man and a woman, acted as godparents and we were told that they would take care of the baby if the parents died or were unable to care for it. Now, in reality godparents usually took a special interest in their godchildren, like giving them presents or money for their birthdays, and that was the part of our godparents that we liked!

My next memory of Catholicism was when our mother introduced the family Rosary. As a very small child I can remember every night after supper at around 7 p.m. we would be ordered to kneel around in the kitchen and say the Rosary. My mother was in charge of this very solemn event and as a child I was absolutely fascinated with her knowledge of the whole thing.

She knew all the different decades of the Rosary but, far more impressively, she also knew all the other prayers associated with the Rosary of that time, like the Hail Holy Queen and the Litany of the Blessed Virgin Mary and the Litany of the Saints: they went on and on for what appeared like hours. Eventually as I got older I was allowed to say a decade of the Rosary: this meant that I played the lead role for one decade.

I started national school in September 1951 and there I was introduced to more prayers by Mrs Agnes Ennis, who was the teacher in charge of the infants. In those days very small children did not go to Mass on Sundays. As far as I can remember I didn't go to Mass until I started school and that was at four years of age. But I can remember more about the journey to Mass than the Mass itself. The reason was that we travelled to Mass in a pony and trap and that was very exciting for me because I loved horses and occasionally my father would allow me to hold the reins and drive the pony. This was the highlight of going to Mass. I guess God was not too happy that driving the horse was more important than him.

At that time in our parish, Bansha and Kilmoyler, in West Tipperary, the local parish priest was a very well-known and famous man: Canon John Hayes. In addition to being our parish priest, he was also the founder of a national organisation. Canon Hayes was a native of Murroe, County Limerick and in 1937 he founded Muintir na Tíre, a national movement that set out to organise the development of local communities throughout rural Ireland. He was born into severe poverty in County Limerick and he dedicated his life to serving the poor, fighting for equality and justice for all. Indeed, in 1946 when he was first appointed parish priest of Bansha and Kilmoyler, one of his very first decisions was to get rid of the practice that allowed rich families and individuals to buy pews in the church for their personal use. Their names would be put on the pew and no other person could sit in that pew even when it was empty. Canon Hayes announced on his very first day that he was ending this practice saying 'in God's house, everyone is equal'. This was seen by most of the parish as a fantastic decision and he became an instant hero. Of course, some of the richer people were not impressed: after all, he had in one go knocked them off their high perch. As a small child I remember listening to his sermons during Mass and while I had no idea what he was talking about I can still recall his voice and his charisma.

As I grew older, I soon realised that Canon Hayes was a unique and very special human being. He died in January, 1957 and I can still remember the news of his death breaking; it was mentioned on the news on Radio Éireann and in those days that was big stuff. Over the years I have read many of his speeches and writings and I have no hesitation in saying that he was indeed a prophet and a man ahead of his time. Over 75 years ago he said that materialism would lead to nothing but greed, selfishness, competition and individualism. He said a community should be a social mix of equals, all caring and sharing for one another. And he said that human beings should not be classified as production machines. If he came back to Ireland during the Celtic Tiger era he would have been astonished to discover that everything he warned against had actually happened. For me Canon Hayes was one of a very small number of individuals that I knew over my lifetime who lived a truly Christian life: he talked the talk and he also walked the walk. He remains one of my great heroes.

I have to mention the annual missions that were held in the parish when I was a child. I remember in the 1950s they often lasted two weeks – Mass every morning with a 'short' sermon of about 30 minutes and then every night the main mission with a sermon that often lasted well over an hour. And most of the missioners preached at the very top of their voices and often put the fear of God into people. Looking back now, they were indeed extraordinary events and they had huge influence, most of it negative, on the lives of people. For example, married couples took their instructions and teaching on procreation very much on board and often as a direct result many had huge families, even though they had not the means to support them. Above all, young women and mothers suffered dreadfully as a result. A young woman who got pregnant outside of marriage was very much ostracised by family, local community and by the Catholic Church. And many mothers believed that they had no choice but to have as many children as God gave them irrespective of the consequences it was having on their own health and well-being. And then as if to rub salt in the mother's wounds she had to be 'churched' after each birth – this was the custom whereby mothers had to wait around after Sunday Mass for the priest to cleanse them of their sin, the sin being 'giving birth'. The whole thing was absolutely crazy.

Back at national school, my first major Catholic event was First Holy Communion in 1954. The teacher, Mrs Ennis, or the mistress as she was called in those days, put a lot of work into preparing the children in first class for this ceremony. The classes were tiny, five or six boys and girls in each class. One of the highlights of preparing for First Holy Communion was when Mrs Ennis drove us to Kilmoyler Church to practise for the big event. And while we were in the church she used to hear our confessions in the confession boxes, our first time in a confessional. And she used to cut paper into round shapes like Communion Hosts and placed them in our mouths with strict instructions not to swallow the paper but, of course, many of us did just that and to say that we got a good telling off is a very mild way of putting it. Another exciting part of First Holy Communion was going into Cahir, our local town, to get a new suit for the occasion. Certainly in my case this was my first ever new suit of clothes and I can still remember going into Gerry Sheehan's drapery shop in the Square in Cahir, where my mother always shopped when she was buying new clothes for us. In those days First Holy Communion was always held on a Saturday and during Mass we received Holy Communion for the first time. It was an occasion that I never forgot and it still brings back very happy memories after almost 60 years.

I was confirmed in 1958 but confirmation never had the same appeal for me as First Holy Communion. I was confirmed in Bansha church – my sister Kathleen was also confirmed on the same day – and overall it was a low-key affair when compared to First Holy Communion.

My next major involvement with the Catholic Church was when I became an altar boy, I think around 1957. I served Mass for a number of years and again I have nothing but very happy memories of that period. The big events at that time were Christmas and the Easter ceremonies. But the other big plus of being an altar boy was that you were asked to serve at funeral

Masses and, best of all, at weddings. Of course, the real reason weddings and funeral Masses were so special was that we got money for performing our serving duties. In those days 10 shillings was a fortune and on rare occasions we might get a pound note; now that was put down as a great wedding.

In recent years, we are all aware that a number of priests have been convicted of the serious sexual abuse of some altar boys and many of the offences were committed 20, 30, 40 and 50 years ago. I must say that during all my time serving as an altar boy I never had any such experience, nor did I ever witness any wrong doing on the part of any of the many priests that I had regular contact with; indeed, the opposite was the case, all the priests being absolute gentlemen towards me and the other servers.

In the mid-1980s I was appointed to the Board of Directors of both Cross Care and Centre Care by Bishop Desmond Williams in Dublin. Cross Care and Centre Care are organisations directly under the auspices of the Dublin Archdiocese and answerable to the Archbishop of Dublin. I served on both boards for many years and the one thing I can say for sure is that these organisations did and continue to do outstanding work serving those in need throughout the Archdiocese of Dublin. But I did learn that church politics plays a huge part in the everyday life of the Catholic Church in Ireland. Indeed, I discovered that there was a close similarity in style and practice between state bureaucracy and Catholic Church bureaucracy. In fact, one thing was very obvious: anyone who didn't toe the party line in either system was soon isolated and usually severely punished. And the church was often even more brutal than the state insofar as a church person had no protection and no public right to fight his or her case. One thing that amazed me was that all the church people that I felt were wronged always accepted the decision of the establishment and continued to serve even if privately they felt wronged or, on occasions, betrayed. And while the church was often preaching the need for justice and forgiveness, these were the last things it applied when dealing with one of its own priests.

After joining the prison service in Limerick in 1968, I was transferred to Shanganagh Castle, Shankill, County Dublin in

1971 and there I met a full-time Catholic chaplain for the first time. Of course there was a chaplaincy service at Limerick prison but it was part-time and mainly consisted of one of the local priests from St John's parish visiting on occasions and celebrating Mass on Sundays. In the late 1960s, Shanganagh Castle was a new innovation as far as Irish prisons were concerned. It was an open prison accommodating up to 65 boys between the ages of 16 and 21 years, it had no physical security like high walls or wire fencing and operated on the basis of trust. The boys were trusted and the vast numbers responded positively and completed their sentences and did not abscond.

Fr Ben Mulligan was the first full-time Catholic chaplain at Shanganagh Castle and he was a most wonderful Christian man. For many years, in addition to filling the role of chaplain, he also acted as a welfare officer, being a counsellor and liaison officer to the boys' families. He was also a great sportsman and played football with the boys and organised football matches and many other recreational events. He did marvellous work and enjoyed excellent relationships with the boys, the staff and the establishment – no mean feat in itself. Anyway, it certainly brought home to me the value and potential of chaplaincy in prisons and from that time onwards I became a total supporter of prison chaplaincy. During all my years working as a prison governor I saw at first hand the wonderful commitment and dedication of prison chaplains, mostly Catholic, but not exclusively because I met wonderful chaplains representing other religions too. I have no hesitation in saying that prison chaplains, nowadays made up of priests, religious sisters and lay people, provide an invaluable and unique service to prisoners and their families and, of course, to prison staff. A senior civil servant in the Department of Justice, Dick Crowe, way back in 1971, said to the staff in Shanganagh Castle: 'If you really want to put your religion into everyday practice, there's no better place to do it than working with young offenders.' I totally agree with him. Prison chaplains are absolute proof of this every day of every week.

My admiration for members of the Catholic Church is not confined exclusively to those who worked as prison chaplains. Because during my life I have met a number of quite extraordinary individuals who lived truly Christian lives. People like Fr Peter McVerry, who has done wonderful work providing care and support for homeless boys in Dublin and, above all, being a strong public advocate on their behalf. Alice Leahy of Trust, who has served the homeless in Dublin city for years and years, Sr Caoimhín Ní Uallacháin, whose work with ex-prisoners and their families in the Ballyfermot area was absolutely phenomenal; the late and great Sr Marie Joseph O'Reilly, who dedicated her life serving those afflicted with addiction; Sr Consilio Fitzgerald of Cuan Mhuire, a truly great Christian; Sr Stan Kennedy of Focus Ireland whose work for the homeless is well known throughout Ireland and beyond, are just a few of the many great individuals that I personally had the privilege of knowing and all of them have been an inspiration to me in my life. The amazing thing is that it was in individuals rather than the Catholic Church as an institution that I found the strongest evidence of Christian values being applied in practice on the ground.

On a personal basis, I'm a total believer in the Christian philosophy. Indeed, I believe that if we could all live by this philosophy, the world would be a much better place. I believe that at the very kernel of Christianity is a requirement to treat every human being with the utmost respect and to ensure that justice and humanity underpin all our dealings with others – basically treat others with the respect that we ourselves expect. Other requirements of the Christian philosophy that I believe are fundamental are forgiveness, compassion, generosity, mercy, kindness and humility. I have no hesitation in saying that it's very difficult, if not impossible, for any human being to live a truly Christian life. I most certainly struggle and fail most of the time. I often recall the observation on Christianity attributed to Ghandi: 'I like your Christ; I don't like your Christians; your Christians are not much like your Christ.' And I'm afraid that's the great challenge for all Catholics. Attending Mass and other ceremonies is the easy bit – the cosmetics really. The difficult bit is living it every day – no need to preach our virtues if we live by them.

Finally, does the Catholic Church as an institution give clear example and leadership and show us how it's done? I'm afraid not. For example, I can find little evidence that shows that the Catholic Church applies the Christian philosophy in its many dealings with its own priests when they have sinned; certainly not enough mercy, forgiveness or compassion. I long for the day when the church as an institution clarifies its position on this. I know full well that to forgive the offending priest won't be popular but being popular was never Christ's way.

I'll finish with a quotation from the Prophet Micah in the Old Testament and which really captures what is expected of all Christians: 'This is what Yahweh asks of you; only this, to act justly, to love tenderly and to walk humbly with your God' (Micah 6:8).

Catholicism: a grand narrative[1]

Marie Murray

I am a Catholic because I was born Catholic. Being Catholic and Irish, or Irish and Catholic, given the almost inextricable link between these two conditions, was an integral part of life in the 1950s Ireland in which I grew up. It was an extraordinary black and white era, literally, emotionally and metaphorically. I recall it still in monochrome images that crackle like Movietone. They are eidetic memories of a Catholic childhood of Proustian power that time cannot erase. I loved Catholicism then. I recall simultaneous awe at its extraordinary beauty and anger at its contradictions: emotions which I realise that I retain to this day as I write these words and remember how every aspect of individual, personal, family, social, community and political life was shaped by Catholicism in the Ireland in which I grew up.

The dichotomies in 1950s Ireland were uncompromising: child or adult, married or single, good or bad, body or soul, rich or poor, right or wrong, Catholic or Protestant. As a backdrop to these polarities lay the greatest chasm of all: the awesome gulf between heaven and hell; locations between which one's immortal soul hung in precarious balance, dependent on the merest transgression in thought or act. As the pendulum swung perilously between perpetual reward and eternal damnation, one could be consigned to either state in a second. Hell for all eternity was a very long time.

Temptation was everywhere. The 'occasions of sin' were numerous – disobedience to parents, teachers and authority high on the list of potential childhood transgressions. While

---

1.   Three meanings are intended in this title. First the Irish colloquial 'grand' means 'great, wonderful, fine', 'an inspirational story', 'the greatest story ever told'. The second colloquial term uses 'grand' as 'behaving in a superior fashion', above others, condescending. The third meaning is that of philosopher Jean-Francois Lyotard in *The Postmodern Condition: A Report on Knowledge* (1979) in which 'grand narratives' are powerful institutional forms of knowledge. Postmodernism is the breaking down of these ideological, institutional, all-powerful narratives in the manner in which the institutional church is looking once more towards the local, the community and the Vatican II ideal of a church of the people.

venial sin stained the soul, mortal sin deprived it of sanctifying grace, blackening it beyond redemption without remediation of the sacrament of confession. The seven deadly sins were of this ilk, amongst them sloth – a concept of languid evil because 'the devil found work for idle hands'.

There were dire warnings impressive to the child's mind about this devil, who roamed 'like a roaring lion seeking whom he may devour',[2] evoking in me a determination not to be tricked by his strategies. It was necessary to be swift of thought and intense in repentance to safeguard one's soul, to know 'the act of contrition'[3] by heart so that it could be annunciated if one found oneself unexpectedly at death's door or to whisper it into the ear of another should you come across them in the final throes of death. This rather bizarre possibility, with which every school child was acquainted, meant that on several occasions, fearing my grandmother to be dead when she fell asleep in her armchair, I recited a full 'act' for her to preserve her immortal soul, although she was perfect in my eyes and I could not reconcile the God of compassion with consigning an elderly woman to burn in the fires of hell forever.

As unbaptised babies were banished to limbo,[4] it was implied that conditional baptism be conducted on any baby who might not have received this sacrament. I personally remember bestowing this zealously at the age of eight with the preface 'if thou art not already baptised I baptise thee' for the babies of family friends or neighbours on the basis of 'to be sure, to be sure'. Catholicism had abundant practices to inspire the idealism of a child in words such as 'to give and not to count the cost, to fight and not to heed the wounds, to toil and not to seek for rest, to labour and to look for no reward',[5] lay heroic possibilities for the 'soldiers of Christ'[6] that outstripped any superheroes that comics could provide at that time.

2. Proverbs 28:15; 1 Peter 5:8.
3. Prayer of sorrow and repentance recited in confession.
4. Originally conceived as a place where the souls of unbaptised babies resided. It has since been relegated to a 'theological hypothesis' in the service of ensuring prompt baptism – a review which angered the many women who had grieved for many years for their stillborn or unbaptised babies whom they believed to have been there deprived of the 'face of God' in limbo.
5. St Ignatius of Loyola.
6. Through the sacrament of confirmation, one became a 'soldier of Christ'.

The stories of the saints, of martyrdom, fortitude, rebellion and grace: of Maria Goretti who died to 'save her virtue' (whatever that meant); Catherine of Sienna's injunction to 'set the world on fire' by being who you were meant to be; St Brigid, *Muire na nGael*; Joan Of Arc's dramatic end; all provided impressive imaginative role-models of feisty women who challenged the authorities of their time. Yet irrespective of how fervently I waited for visions and apparitions or for large-winged angels to bring direct messages from God, or for Our Lady to appear to me with injunctions to pray, as she did to the children of Lourdes and Fatima, no such visitations were made. Perhaps they were reserved for candidates of a humbler disposition than those, like me, who scanned their hands with hope for signs of the stigmata.[7]

In Ireland half a century ago, faith formation was 'taught' like other 'subjects' on the curriculum, sadly too often with a harshness that denied its message of love; a paradox that did not escape a child's sensibilities. I recall being personally appalled at a teacher's anger at a classmate during preparation for confirmation who struggled with the concept of transubstantiation.[8] Moral certitude, *Zeitgeist* of that time, was prescriptive, unquestioning and committed to memory. Truths were irrefutable. Imperatives were categorical. The church was infallible.

So complete was rote inculcation of doctrinal catechesis in early childhood that to this day the answer to the questions from the old 'catechism' can be triggered in me with the reflexivity of Pavlovian conditioning. Ask me any stimulus question from that 'marvellous compendium', to quote G.K. Chesterton, and you will receive a conditioned refrain embedded in the brain 50 years or more ago. Who made the world? God made the world. Who is God? God is Our Father in Heaven, the Creator

---

7. The stigmata were the duplicate wounds of Jesus' crucifixion that were believed to appear on the hand and feet and sometimes on the side of those chosen for this marking by virtue of their 'holiness'.

8. As I recall from that time, the issue was that even if 'receiving' under one species alone, such as bread that it was still the Body, Blood, Soul and Divinity of Jesus Christ under the appearance of bread – now when I view the conceptual requirements made of children at, for example, Piagetian pre-operational and operational stages as we were when learning these tenets, I am amazed at the extent to which we appropriated what was inherently complex.

and Lord of all things. On Pentecost or Whit Sunday, 10 days after the Ascension, the Holy Ghost descended on the apostles in the form of tongues of fire. When should we pray? We should pray very often but especially on Sundays and Holy Days, every morning and every night and in all dangers, temptations and afflictions. The incantations of memory reverberate to the present day with all the power and the glory of when they were first learned in school. With Skinnerian[9] exactitude they are evoked by the tiniest cue, alongside lines of poetry, Latin verbs, enunciation of 'times tables', memorisation of the rivers of Ireland, lines of spellings and the dangers of split infinitives; all indented indelibly in the neurology of mind.

My parents were devout without obsession. They 'observed' what was required, by inclination and coincidental with Catholicism they were upright, honest, decent and 'charitable' in an understated way. There was adherence to rule and ritual which provided me with that mesmerising experience – the Catholic childhood – with evening Rosary, weekly confession, Mass attendance, First Fridays, observance of fast and abstinence, novenas, retreats, dousing with holy water going in and out of church, the mark of ashes on the forehead ('Remember that dust thou art') and the annual calendar of activities that were part of most homes at that time or kept silent about if they were not.

But my parents were equally respectful of those of other faiths at a time in Ireland distinguished by intolerance and for that I am grateful. A funeral, regardless of in whose place of worship it occurred, was attended. The country was traversed to be there, my father finding funerals the ideal way to remain connected to extended family and to a non-materialistic perspective on life. I accompanied him often, watching the discrete presence of the undertakers, their simultaneous assistance and invisibility, tiptoeing around the fragility of the bereaved and the shuffle of the attendees who murmured tongue-tied compassion, sympathy and sorrow, conscious of the ineptitude of

---

9.   Psychologist B.F. Skinner contributed to the stimulus–reward debate with his 'operant conditioning' model proposing that behaviour when it is rewarded or reinforced, is exclusively shaped by environment over which the individual had no control.

words.[10] Then and now, the Catholic funeral had the power and promise of redemption: 'Be not afraid, I go before you'; and whether attendance be perfunctory or social, it is a ritual more resistant to change, perhaps, than customs around other life-cycle[11] events. The November meditations on the 'communion of saints'[12] and the 'souls in purgatory' in addition to partial or plenary indulgences on their behalf may no longer be expressed in the walk in and out and around the churches, but an atavistic consciousness of communion with those who have died remains culturally imbued.

Looking back, it was my grandmother who instilled in me an appreciation of the intellectual wealth in Catholicism. I fell in love with its vocabulary, its vivid visual imagery, the glow of the sanctuary lamp; the fragrant swing of the thurible,[13] the sacredness of silence, the shadows of light and candlelight flickering on the statues in the alcoves of the church, the hush and humility during Exposition[14] and the radiant glitter of the monstrance.[15] The litanies of Benediction remain with me by rote: 'Blessed be God; Blessed be his holy name; Blessed be Jesus Christ true God and true man.' I recall the reverberation of the organ, the haunt of *Tantum Ergo*,[16] singing in the children's choir *Credo in Unum Deum*,[17] the protraction of the *Kyrie Elison*,[18] the *Salve Regina*,[19] the symbolism of *Agnus Dei*,[20] the soothing power of Gregorian Chant and a sense of belonging to

10. This is most poignantly conveyed by poet Seamus Heaney in his poem 'Mid-term break'.
11. Life-cycle is presented most comprehensively by B. Carter and M. McGoldrick (eds), *The Expanded Family Life Cycle: Individual, Family and Social Perspectives* (Allyn and Bacon, 2005).
12. Church triumphant in those who had died and gone to heaven. A distinction between those who had died and gone to heaven, the souls in purgatory still engaged in the expiation of sin, and the faithful on earth.
13. The metal censer suspended from chains, in which incense is burned.
14. The Sacred Host removed from the tabernacle and placed in the monstrance for Eucharistic Adoration purposes.
15. A gold container for the consecrated Host when it is placed on the altar for Eucharistic Adoration.
16. Gregorian Chant – mandated for Benediction of the Blessed Sacrament – written by St Augustine, it is the final stanzas of the Pange Lingua.
17. I believe in One God.
18. The ancient name for the penitential rite, Lord have mercy.
19. The Hail Holy Queen.
20. Before Holy Communion – The Lamb of God.

something that 'always was, always is and always will be', to time and eternity and the privilege of belief.

In a time of material deprivation, when possessions were few and entirely utilitarian, devotional objects were bright and beautiful. They were the 'bling' of times past: the glitter of crystal Rosary beads in a blue silk purse, the mother of pearl bound missal with pages tissue-thin, the delicacy of the mantilla, the miraculous medal on its shimmering chain, golden icons in tiny triptych, and my grandmother's knotted beads in her gnarled hands in incontrovertible belief in the afterlife.

Devotion also brought Renaissance art miniaturised on holy pictures, prayer cards and missal markers: Botticelli's 'Adoration of the Magi' and 'Madonna of the Magnificat', Titian's 'Assumption of the Virgin', 'Christ Carrying the Cross', Fra Angelico's 'Annunciation', Leonardo da Vinci's 'Virgin of the Rocks', Giotto's 'Flight into Egypt', Raphael's 'Cherubini' and the 'realistic mysticism' of Caravaggio's work of the Divine made human,[21] all of which were magnificent to the eyes of a child.

I remember the Tridentine Mass[22] and its mysterious impenetrability and I felt a loss I could not put words on as a child when it changed into 'ordinary' vernacular. I remember regular prayers with wonderful words – 'Turn then most gracious advocate thine eyes of mercy toward us.'[23] There was prostrating and pleading and beseeching for clemency, intercessions sought, 'mourning and weeping in this valley of tears' and meditations on the mysteries of the Rosary so that we might 'imitate what they maintain and obtain what they promise'. The Litany of the Blessed Virgin Mary, each incantation punctuated with a persistent hypnotic 'pray for us' was mesmerising: 'Mirror of Justice, pray for us; Seat of Wisdom, pray for us; Cause of our Joy, pray for us; Spiritual Vessel, pray for us; Vessel of Honour, pray for us; Mystical Rose, pray for us; Tower of David, pray for us; Tower of Ivory, pray for us, House of

---

21. Noteworthy in Irish history's relationship with religious art was the discovery of the Caravaggio *The Taking of Christ* in the dining room of the Jesuit House in Leeson Street in Dublin.
22. The Traditional Latin Mass before the Second Vatican Council after which the text was altered.
23. The Salve Regina.

Gold, pray for us; Ark of the Covenant, pray for us; Gate of Heaven, pray for us; Morning Star, pray for us.'

As I reflect back on that time now, I see the enormous impact that such litanies had on me, because despite the critiques since then of an outdated doctrinal approach, despite the routine chanting of Latin words whose translation was withheld, despite the unashamed inculcation of incantations into young minds, with rituals that were absent of apparent meaning and repetition of the incomprehensible, I think we were also a generation that was privileged. We were allowed to enter into language realms from which the current child is excluded in a 'dumbed-down world' that reveres the common denominator in the mistaken belief that less is inclusive. Diminution excludes all and respects none. The intellect of the child in the past was respected and bestowed with a vocabulary and symbolism that exceeded comprehension, awakening aesthetic sensibilities, 'analogical imagination'[24] and allegorical appreciation and providing impetus to a generation of artists, poets, writers and thinkers[25] and a deep yearning for the transcendent.

If one wonders what has evoked the frenetic popularity of the Harry Potter novels, one hypothesis is that they opened up a world of magic and mystery, good and evil, concept and vocabulary, similar to that which was once provided by formal religion and in doing so met an unfulfilled need in the postmodern child. While we may deplore the blind, intolerant certitude of mid-twentieth century Ireland and rightly so, and while we recognise that its teaching methods took little account of the developmental status or psychology of the child, we might equally question the moral relativity now offered to children, depriving them of the security of boundaries, the surety of beliefs and the ethics of beneficence.

But there were contradictions from the past that wounded too. Ireland half a century ago was not a place of nuance, shade

---

24. See Andrew Greeley, *The Catholic Myth* (New York: Simon and Schuster, 1990).

25. Consider the extent of Catholic imagery in the work of James Joyce, Samuel Beckett, John McGahern, Brian Moore, Kate O'Brien. Frank O' Connor's 'My First Confession' is a classic, as are the evocations of Catholicism in the poetry of Patrick Kavanagh.

or tolerance. The dominant Jansenist[26] Catholic and nationalistic discourse of 1950s Ireland was maintained by public display, private worship and social retribution for those who stepped outside its structures.[27] In a post-colonial society, this new hegemonic ascendency of church and state was oppressive for many, especially women about whom an inappropriate idealisation[28] was created. Girls were indeed 'poor banished children of Eve', subject to humiliating discrimination that did not permit them to go beyond the altar rails, to serve at Mass, to touch the Host, or to assume roles other than docility in the face of canonical suspicion towards women who seemed to be simultaneously revered and feared in the ambivalence of virgin-mother ideals. It was a patriarchal, hubristic hierarchy in which women and children were on the lowest rung.[29]

I do not know if my mother was offended by not being worthy to venture past the altar rails, but I was shamed and angered as a child and insulted on her behalf as an adult. While I had no vocabulary then with which to articulate my disappointment in the discrepancies I observed in Irish life, at a visceral level the hypocrisy of adults disturbed me with that acute sense of injustice which is the particular province of childhood and outrage in the child. I remain unimpressed with the attitude towards women that continues in the church today, encapsulated in the ban on debate about the ordination of women. Any institution that prohibits dialogue damages itself.

---

26. Jansenism after Cornelius Jansen (1585–1638), Bishop of Ypres, characterised by moral severity and position on grace from Augustine. Included the idea of the total sinfulness of humanity, predestination, and the need for Christians to rely upon a faith in God which human reason cannot validate. Some accept that Ireland was Jansenistic while others reject that; but those who remember mid-twentieth century Ireland will recall that disposition especially with regard to women.

27. The institutional structures that share common values. In social constructionism the way interest groups exercise power through particular 'communicative practices'. (See seminal writings of psychologists John Shotter, 1989 and Kenneth Gergen, 1992.)

28. Within psychology 'idealisation' often involves splitting into good/bad. The virgin/tart dichotomy which excludes the reality of ordinary women is one such example.

29. See P. Glick and S.T. Fiske, 'An Ambivalent Alliance: Hostile and Benevolent Sexism as Complementary Justifications for Gender Inequality', in *American Journal of Psychology*, 56(2), 2001, pp. 109–18.

Yet despite frequent exasperation and occasional dismay, I continue to be a Catholic and to remain connected to that tradition with love and belief in its God. Perhaps if I were to dig deep I might find that the choice I made of psychology as a profession (described to me in the Ireland of 1970 as a godless choice!) was a vocation rather than a career, a privilege more than a profession, and a 'calling' borne out of the mental milieu in which I grew up. I think that it arose in some unconscious realm out of the concept of the confessional, the power of words to heal, a belief in being with those in pain, opportunity to understand suffering, to confront the mysteries of the mind, to uncover meaning and 'to give and not to count the cost'.

Looking back on the past, I lived in a time that did not know how rapidly change would overtake it, how imminent was its end, how indelibly it would inscribe itself into the heart and soul of a generation and how painful future ruptures of attachment would be.[30]

I never did receive the stigmata! Yet I think I got to see the wounds of Christ in those who were depressed, those who felt helpless and hopeless, those who needed to know that they were valued and valuable, so that when I had no further psychological skill to offer I prayed that they would be okay. I was never granted those apparitions that my child's heart desired but in my work I have glimpsed, especially in those most damaged, the countenance of the Divine. So that I believe, not with the rationality of science, not because I need Freud's 'illusory crutch' nor Jung's 'indispensable spiritual support' nor even Victor Frankl's 'profoundly personalised' search for ultimate meaning, but rather with a very simple faith in a religion that has at its core the command 'that you have love, for one another'. That's good enough for me.

---

30. The tragedy of the mishandling of so many issues needs no reiteration here.

Growing into Catholicism

Rónán Mullen

One of the advantages of repeating sixth class in national school was that one got to feel important for a while. That meant different things to different children. But one thing I recall is being chief Mass server whenever the station Masses took place in my own station area or in one of the areas nearby. Not every Catholic had the experience of growing up in an area where station Masses were said, so a quick explanation may be needed. Each parish in our diocese was divided into station areas. There would be a spring and autumn Mass in a different house in each area, so that (in our case anyway) the 'stations' came around every six or seven years. This was a big deal, not least because it was often with a focus on the forthcoming stations that much needed renovating, repairs or painting finally got done at home. (Especially if the householder was a builder. It was once widely believed that builders neglected to maintain their own houses while sorting out everybody else's problems. I believe it was true in some cases.)

There were at least three reasons for an altar boy to look forward to a station Mass: time off school, a couple of pounds earned, but most of all a good feed afterwards. How I loved to hear the whistle of a kettle and the clatter of cups as the priest collected the 'dues' after the Mass. Because no matter how much the priest urged that 'a cup of tea' was all that was expected, a lot of trouble went in at the hospitality end for the stations. It was a bit patriarchal by today's standards because the priest, the man of the house, some of the neighbouring men and the Mass server would all be served at table, while everyone else celebrated more informally around the house. The upside of sitting in was that you felt important. The downside, if there was one, was that one might miss out on the full *à la carte* menu. Mass servers worried about those kinds of things.

But of all the station Masses I ever served, I remember one in particular because I learned a valuable lesson. It was in one of those higgledy-piggledy houses where no room was very big and people gathered in nooks and crannies to hear the Mass. The parish priest, Fr Joe Smyth of Ahascragh, asked for a head-count for Holy Communion. The job wasn't done very well. It emerged, during Communion, that we were badly short. Now the parish priest was a really good man, a wise and compassionate person who became a kind mentor to me in my teenage years. But he could be cranky. As he began to mutter in annoyance, I spotted the cardboard box of unconsecrated Hosts and I offered them to him so that he could top up his ciborium. Fr Smyth was aghast. I can still hear him hiss, in sorrow and desperation, 'Is that all you know?'

I don't think anybody heard and I don't recall feeling embarrassed. And I don't know what the people who wrote *Walk in Love* or *Alive-O* or those who now oversee the teaching of religion in our schools would have expected of a boy of 12 or 13. But I remember Fr Smyth's disappointment. I would have been one of the more interested students when he visited our school. He always encouraged us to ask questions about the faith, and not to be afraid to wonder. I always responded with enthusiasm. But despite his best efforts and mine, how the Eucharist – source and summit of the life of the church – came about, had passed right over my head.

I didn't realise the import of it at the time but that moment has often served as a personal reminder of how people can have an easy familiarity with the church, its structures, culture and norms, its personnel and its architecture, and still never get to the heart or essence of it. Weren't many of us, in a sense, 'vaccinated' against life in the church? We know that 'through a chink too wide, there comes in no wonder', but perhaps we saw so much of the church that we missed what was really there. Is this why many Irish Catholics feel embarrassed when some of their number appear to believe in the church a little too much, or act as if God actually existed and loved them? Is it also part of the reason why people who encounter controversy, contradiction and serious scandal in the church often feel a strong urge to disengage and leave unexplored the great questions which the church is there to help them explore and ultimately answer?

The recent surveys carried out by the Association of Catholic Priests and *The Irish Times* may bear out the vaccination theory: a majority of self-described Catholics manifestly reject core church teachings such as the Real Presence of Christ in the Eucharist. This is very significant since what the church teaches about the Eucharist is at the core of its mission in this world.

But the surveys don't tell us why people reject the teaching. Is it because they have considered the church's 'take' on the Eucharist, but do not find it plausible? Or do they reject something they have never really heard or never had taught to them? Have they ever really internalised St Augustine's idea that we 'become what we receive', that as we take Christ's body into our physical selves, we are in fact absorbed by him and become gradually more Christ than ourselves? And if people have gone through 20, 30, 40 or more years of familiarity with the church up to now, without hearing any of this, can they, at this stage, find the freshness, eagerness or curiosity to explore and try to live it?

Though I don't know of any specific survey to back it up, I have little doubt that there is a strong correlation between those Catholics who do believe in doctrines such as transubstantiation and those who are more likely to earnestly and sincerely ponder their faith in their heart. To put it another way, Catholics who attend Mass in the fullest sense (who are more than physically present at Mass), who try to have a living prayer life, and who see in scripture the inspired word of God, are much more likely to search for, and discover, the deep truth in the church's authoritative teaching, no matter what the subject of that teaching is.

My growing awareness that there were significant gaps in my religious knowledge led me to appreciate the importance of faith's intellectual dimensions. It's one thing coming to this realisation, though, and another thing to act on it. I was lucky to have positive influences to help me. I have already mentioned Fr Joe Smyth who, for years after the Communion outrage, shared his knowledge with me and encouraged me to think deeper. There were other things too, like the inspiring retreats and courses put on by the Elphin Diocese in Donamon Pastoral

Centre, an excellent secondary school education where the principal and staff had a Christian commitment and a deep sense of the dignity of each person. But most of all, there was the loving and supportive role which my family played in my faith formation. And that was just in my teenage years. Later years brought new friends, fellow students, inspiring causes, wise work colleagues, encounters with different traditions and styles within the Catholic family, all helping me to keep trust in God and joy in life despite the inevitable frustrations, fears, inadequacies, setbacks and disappointments.

As common as my own story is, it is hardly universal. I realise that many Irish children grew up with a different experience of the Catholic faith. I recall chatting to a French agnostic friend a number of years ago about our different perspectives on life. It was the kind of conversation that makes Irish people deeply uncomfortable unless it takes place inside a public house after 11 p.m. at night but which foreigners find completely normal. 'Unlike you, Rónán,' my friend said, 'I wasn't brought up in the love of God.' I was touched by the generosity of his assessment and struck by the realisation that his description of my experience was true. I have often wondered how many Irish could say that about their experience of Catholicism. Would many not use definitions like 'love of rules' or 'fear of God' instead of 'love of God'? And here, I believe, is what has saved me to date from the vaccination of over-familiarity against life in the church. Yes, it was the intellectual guidance from various quarters in the years following my exposure as a heretic at the station Mass. But much more importantly, I was taught to love God as a real person who accompanies me now as I struggle to write this. That has made the difference. A God who took on human form to enter human history to establish a communion of love with his children; who waits for me in a fuller way at the end of my time on earth. This is a very particular take on religion, and an overwhelmingly positive thing to have received. If I describe this view as something that happened to me, because of people I've known and events that occurred, it's because that's how I experienced it. But I believe God's grace operates through the hearts and hands of his willing creatures and through the events of their lives.

I have others to thank for my experiences, and ultimately God. From the religious vision of life that was shared with me, I caught the sense of my own dignity as a human being. Part of this dignity is an appreciation that as members of the human race, we have been given reason to help us search for the truth about life and living, and the truth about God too. Many of the people I've admired were not just people of faith, but people of reason too. They combined sharp and untiring minds with a real sense that faith is a gift.

While my faith journey into adulthood was a positive one, it wasn't without its difficulties. Going to university and being away from home brought new fear and stress into my life. Like most young people coming from a world where faith was welcomed and nourished and then being transplanted into a world where scepticism had a real foothold, I questioned my faith in a new way. This time it was a more existential, painful type of questioning. I worried whether I could sustain my faith into the future and whether, even if I could, it would be something worth sustaining and not just a comfort blanket for my life. My mentors in faith had taught me to think independently and to ask questions, so there could be no case of putting questions aside simply because they made me uncomfortable. Without managing to prove or disprove the existence of God, I learned to deal with the challenge. I chose to believe because I knew it was a reasonable thing to do and my heart was attracted by it. The search for wisdom, truth and love should be everything in a person's life and it became more, not less, possible if you tried to live out your relationship with a loving God.

The particular social circles in which I immersed myself helped resolve tensions between my personal faith and the wider world as I experienced it. It is sometimes easy to overlook the huge influence our environment has on us, whether it be friends, family, media or culture. I saw how others integrated their new experiences into their faith and how they resolved tensions between the two without either denying their faith or dismissing the secular world. 'Let there be no compulsion in religion', says the Koran.

This is precisely how I have experienced Catholicism in my engagement with those closest to me. Going from school to college to the world of work, including a period working in the Communications Office of the Dublin Archdiocese, I have been constantly challenged, by and through the impressive people I've met, to recognise the deep wisdom in church teaching. The experience for many other people had a different structure; they got an early and short (and often superficial) immersion in church teaching, only to see it exposed to cynicism, criticism and apathy thereafter.

Catholicism must be an affair of both the head and the heart. The church's teaching on social issues always struck me as intellectually credible and socially relevant. But especially now. Like others, I reject the easy, reactionary consensus against any church teaching that challenges an absolutist picture of individual freedom and a maximalist view of satisfaction. But what would I have been like if I grew up in the 1950s when the lazy consensus, we are told, went in the other direction, that is to say, in favour of all things associated with the Catholic Church? Would I have been conformist or non-conformist? Any certainty in answering such questions can never be honest. I hope my Catholicism is based on principle – and yet I am well aware of how strong is the pull of social conformity. The art critic Harold Rosenberg captured it well with the title of one of his most famous essays, 'The Herd of Independent Minds'. I hope I'd have had the grace and ability to be sceptical of a Catholicism that was too institutionally comfortable and didn't always offer coherence and compassion.

As a politician in early-twenty-first century Ireland, I seem to spend a lot of time explaining that some of the values I speak about – respect for life from the moment of conception, the importance of marriage between a man and a woman as a key element of a healthy society, the importance of respecting the spiritual search and the religious and ethical convictions of Christian families in our education system – shouldn't just make sense to Catholics or Christians, but should also be compelling to other believers, as well as to non-believers. I seem to spend a lot of time promoting a rational alliance between people of faith and people of different faith, weaker faith or no faith, in order to uphold public support for certain key values.

Sometimes I think that no matter how hard one tries, people

aren't very concerned about whether the argument makes sense or not. When one listens to debates on the TV and radio, one starts to think that most people may be like that. It's not what's logical that determines whether they agree – it's the gut feeling they have.

But say not the struggle naught availeth

The Christian must speak about trying to be a Christian, through words and a lifestyle that proclaim that God IS, that God reigns in human hearts, that God has loved humanity into existence, that all this can make sense of our lives, that it gives us a meaning and a purpose, that it gives us a reason and a way to cope with all the challenges that life can possibly throw at us, a willingness to grapple with the mystery of suffering, an understanding of the potential of suffering, and an indestructible optimism about our destiny. Maybe, if we can get across all that, the political and social values we believe in will be more attractive to people of all faiths and none.

But in the meantime, the Christian people of the world have to encourage believers to see sense in what they believe, and non-believers to see the natural truth and reasonableness in the values that Christians try to promote, especially when important public policy choices depend on our respect for these values. Seeing the deep wisdom of church teaching is easier on some issues than on others. Most people 'get' the teaching on abortion, whether they agree with it or not. Human equality is the cornerstone of human rights and is contingent upon simply being human, not on being a strong or intelligent or powerful human. The same theology is at the heart of church teaching on how the sanctity of human life shapes our view of the death penalty, torture, prostitution, social welfare, disability, trafficking and euthanasia. Also, regardless of whether a person accepts the church's conclusion on these issues, he or she can usually detect a coherent structure for thinking out the moral truths that flow from the idea of a human being made in the image of God.

But contemporary society finds it much more difficult to grasp the rationale for church teaching on contraception, for instance. The teaching is more nuanced and delicate in this case, while some of its presuppositions are radically at odds with the spirit of the times. The idea of openness to human life being a basic good, and sexuality transcending mere physical enjoyment to signify an everlasting commitment between two persons, a commitment uniting them as one on all levels of their being, especially bodily – these teachings are sublime but tragically vulnerable in a world sceptical of any relationship with God as central to personal well-being. Many Catholics struggle with the teaching as well. Yet, if there is a loving God, notions of human autonomy and privacy cannot be enough – they are too self-centred to encapsulate the deep meaning of right action in a complex world. These notions are too two-dimensional; they lack the transcendent beauty that the Christian proposal inspires. The human being closed off from God has nowhere to go but towards the satisfaction of his or her own desires. Christianity invites us to think about God and the meaning of our bodies and what God created us for: an eternal as well as temporal reality. Modern Catholics shouldn't be surprised that the church's teaching here is deeply controversial and widely unpopular. Sex is a cultural battleground because our entire understanding of ourselves is at stake.

Most of what I've written here has to do with my personal response to the proposal of Catholic faith. But faith must have its public side too. I have encountered many people, thinking liberals and fair-minded agnostics, who see the importance of the church's contribution to major public debates. They see in Catholic social teaching a strong intellectual content available for all persons of goodwill to digest.

The church in Ireland has a mixed record in how it has gone about presenting this social teaching. It continues to lead the way in working with the poor, elderly and disabled, while it sometimes stands alone in defending the rights of unborn persons. All this good work stands in stark contrast to how it has dealt, on occasions, with vulnerable children in residential care and those who became victims of child abusers. There is a danger now that the shame and exhaustion caused by these scandals might undermine the church's confidence in the work it must do. Misguided friends urge the church to jettison its more challenging social teachings in an effort to restore its lost popularity. People with other agendas sense all this, and increasingly we hear their voices calling for the church to be silent and to remove itself from all aspects of public life. They use the church's past failures to justify their present attitude. They paint the church as symbolising and causing all that was and is bad in Irish society. In the Seanad (the Upper House of the Irish Parliament) in July 2012, the Minister for Education, Ruairí Quinn, discussed institutional abuse and asked, 'Why did observant Catholics in the civil service, in the Department of Education and elsewhere, feel so compelled that, in some cases, they were not prepared to act?' Had the Minister any evidence that such neglect and inaction were because of, rather than despite, people's Catholicism? It doesn't appear so, because as he then said, 'This has been speculated on because we can only imagine. I am not quoting any document or evidence.'

But it is up to the church and all its people to prove these sceptics wrong for the sake of God's plan for humanity and the well-being of society. We need increased conviction in the gospel message and the teaching of Christ's church, a conviction that can only convince when we love each other as God loves us.

Growing older, I have realised that the church message was much more impressive than I ever thought before. I have learned that this doesn't make living according to the gospel any easier. My understanding is inadequate, and my will is deficient. But for the progress I have made, and the good it has done me, and the joy I have known, I feel a deep debt of gratitude to all those who have guided me along the way. I owe them more prayers than I will ever manage to say.

Returning to the simple core

Michael Kelly

To write about what Catholicism means to me is a risky business. I have spent the past 10 years writing about Catholicism for a living. The 'signs of the times' that I have tried to interpret, understand and explain have been largely marked by the abuse scandals that, as Pope Benedict XVI poignantly observed, 'have obscured the light of the gospel to a degree that not even centuries of persecution succeeded in doing' (*Pastoral Letter to the Catholics of Ireland*, 19 March 2010). Those words send a chill down my spine every time I read them or hear them spoken.

I have spent the last 10 years listening to people's hopes and anxieties about the church in Ireland. I have been deeply moved and honoured as people have welcomed me into their life of fragile faith.

To be part of the story of the church in Ireland today is to be associated with liars, child abusers, those who covered-up abuse and hypocrites of every description. But it is also to stand on the shoulders of the giants of the Irish church: the saints of old, the heroic missionaries who left everything to bring the hope and liberation of the gospel to far-flung parts of the globe, the heroic women and men religious who brought life and living to communities during troubled days.

Carlo Carretto, the great Italian spiritualist (1910–88), captures it well when he writes a tribute to the church:

How much I must criticise you, my church,
and yet how much I love you!

You have made me suffer more than anyone
and yet I owe more to you than to anyone.

I should like to see you destroyed
and yet I need your presence.

You have given me much scandal
and yet you alone have made me understand holiness.

Never in this world have I seen anything
more obscurantist, more compromised, more false,
yet never have I touched anything
more pure, more generous or more beautiful.

Countless times
I have felt like slamming the door of my soul in your face
– and yet, every night,
I have prayed that I might die in your arms!

No, I cannot be free of you, for I am one with you,
even if not completely you.

Then too – where should I go?
To build another church?
But I cannot build another church without the same defects,
for they are my own defects.

And again, if I were to build another church,
it would be my church, not Christ's church.

No, I am old enough. I know better!

I cannot remember a time in my life where Catholicism was not central. I grew up in the 1980s in an instinctively Catholic family in a strong Catholic community where the parish church was at the heart of the community.

The part of rural west Tyrone that formed and forged me has a long Christian tradition and had suffered dearly for loyalty to the Catholic faith. Not far from my home was the Mass rock of Corradinna where my ancestors huddled together in a hidden glen for the celebration of the Eucharist during Penal persecution. Those same people who eked out a meagre existence from an ungenerous land knew the vitality that the Bread of Life gives and the centrality of the Eucharist. They knew that the Eucharist was the 'source and summit' of the Christian life centuries before the Second Vatican Council said so.

From when I was a young boy I was mesmerised – haunted even – by the many stories of heroism and bravery that surround the Mass rock at Corradinna, and indeed the many sites around Ireland that paradoxically incorporate rugged beauty and a history of religious persecution, the devastation of the famine and at the same time beautiful places of pilgrimage.

Above all – though I wouldn't have known how to articulate it at the time – I was mightily impressed by the witness that there are things worth making a sacrifice for. In his song *Imagine*, John Lennon spoke rather glibly about his hope of creating a world where there was nothing to live or die for. It strikes me as a rather empty idea of the world. No, my forbearers knew that there are things worth making a sacrifice for, things worth living and dying for, and I was impressed by that.

It is of these people that I think when I hear Pope Benedict XVI speak of how the scandals 'have obscured the light of the gospel to a degree that not even centuries of persecution succeeded in doing'.

Mine was a childhood steeped in Catholicism: a Catholicism which combined religious devotion with a lively social action and concern for the marginalised. Groups like the Society of St Vincent de Paul flowed very naturally from the religious life of the community. Priests played a very important role as community leaders. This was particularly true during the darker days of the civil conflict in the North that is often euphemistically called 'the Troubles'. The church and priests, it seems to me, represented the voices of sanity, on the one hand condemning the discrimination faced by many in the Catholic community while maintaining that the campaign of violence by the Provisional IRA (Irish Republican Army) was wrong.

Community was – and is – central to my understanding of Catholicism. 'The joys and the hopes, the griefs and the anxieties' in the wider world of which *Gaudium et Spes* speaks were certainly the bits and pieces in the life of my childhood parish.

Having grown up in the North of Ireland, I am conscious that my experiences of Catholicism have been profoundly different from the experiences of many people who grew up in the southern part of the island of Ireland. I'm frequently bemused, sometimes a little annoyed, when I hear southern Catholics – some of whom have never been to Northern Ireland – lecture me about how my faith has more to do with identity than religion.

All faith has to do with identity. I cannot see faith and life in a dualistic way as if there are different parts of my life that can be turned on and off. I cannot extricate a part of myself that is not an Irish Catholic or, perhaps more precisely, a northern Catholic.

I'm grateful to have been brought up in a part of Ireland where there was not a symbiosis between church and state. It seems to me that the post-independence experience of the Free State profoundly damaged Irish Catholicism and inflicted a deep wound on both the church and the wider society. Having lived in the south of Ireland for the past 15 years, I see up-close-and-personal a society that struggles to renegotiate the relationship between church and state in an often juvenile fashion.

I am not in any way downplaying or minimising the effects on Irish society of a dictatorial style of church governance or the debilitating moralism and hypocrisy which marked twentieth-century Irish Catholicism, but it is my view that cooler heads than now prevail are needed to realign the relationship.

Anti-Catholic sentiment in Ireland dominates discourse about the Catholic Church. Church-bashing has replaced 'Brit-bashing' in the national psyche. Back in the days when nationalism of a certain type, a one-eyed type of nationalism, was very strong in Ireland, if one did not go along with the most vitriolic criticisms of Britain, one was a 'West Brit'. Can it be that we Irish have psychologically replaced this with a very unthinking one-eyed critique of Catholicism?

Sadly, Irish Catholicism has become a very fractious thing too. Disagreements are inevitable, healthy even, but Irish Catholicism has become all too fond of name-calling and crude caricatures. Catholics are becoming Balkanised, throwing terms like right-wing or left-wing at each other. Much as people on either side of what one perceptive American commentator describes as the 'culture wars' within the church would like to believe otherwise, name-calling and caricatures have become endemic.

One of the valuable insights I gain from my work is visiting different parts of the country and experiencing different groups within the church. I can attend self-styled conservative gatherings and hear 'liberals' being denounced ferociously. I can also attend self-styled liberal events and hear 'conservatives' lambasted with equal vitriol.

There are those – on all sides – who wish to exclude everyone whose views they disagree with from the church. Some conservatives say that people who don't like the church's teaching should just leave. Some liberals will say that they are impatient for the sort of changes they want to see in the church yet they see no room in their new church for those who don't want those changes. All the while, the church and faith remain largely irrelevant for most young people and many Irish people live their lives as if God doesn't exist. And yet, this is the church: a church which, despite it all, I go on loving and finding God in.

The late Cardinal Cahal Daly wrote a book in 1998 which he called a 'snapshot' of memories and reflections 'of a long and happy life'. In the Epilogue of that book he wrote:

> This is emphatically not a time for discouragement … or fear about the future … I find myself … wishing that I were young again … and facing today's new challenges with … energy and enthusiasm!

However, while optimistic about the future, Cardinal Daly was also realistic about our times. Quoting John Henry Newman, he noted that in spite 'of bright promise and budding hopes, yet withal, of keen blasts and cold showers and sudden storms'.

It's no exaggeration to say that our recent experience as Catholics in Ireland has been one of 'keen blasts and cold showers and sudden storms'. It has almost become a cliché to speak of the church in Ireland in crisis. But, we have to accept that today the church in Ireland is in a crisis; many say a crisis of credibility, others, a crisis of leadership, and some, a crisis of faith.

Unlike many others both inside and outside the church, I do not chronicle the crisis in Irish Catholicism with any glee. There are those rebels of a bygone era who are now doyens of the Establishment and yet act and write as if they are still challenging a powerful church.

So, in the midst of this what does Catholicism mean to me? Where does my Catholicism sit in the midst of this crisis? Tired? Weary? Deflated? Yes. Hopeful? Optimistic? Joyful? Yes. There are so many constituencies in the church in Ireland today. We need to move beyond constituency, we need to move beyond left and right, beyond liberal and conservative and calibrate ourselves with the gospel of Jesus Christ. We need to again find that beauty and richness of Catholicism that has the power to transform minds and hearts.

When I am deflated, whether it is about the scandals in the church or the fractious infighting that dents our ability to witness to the saving message of Jesus, it is to that Christ-child of Bethlehem that I turn. The wonder of the incarnation transforms our ideas about power and about God. He contrasts the noisy and ostentatious power of this world with the defenceless power of love.

It is above all in the Eucharist, in the breaking of bread, where I feel this power, this love. It is here that I experience and witness the transformative power of God to overcome my human weaknesses and accept that there are weaknesses and divisions in the church, as in any institution. It is here that I am again compelled by a God who draws near to us to help, heal, listen and love.

If we as Irish Catholics, collectively and individually, can regain this sense and the sense of excitement that is the gauntlet of Christian living we will have a church renewed and rebuilt. Not a church built on power or structures, but a church built on love and witness – a church that will have something to offer and say to a changed and changing world. Come Holy Spirit!

The church and me

Gerry Carew

Man cannot understand without images – Thomas Aquinas

When I was a child, my family and I attended St Patrick's parish church in Doon, County Limerick and every Sunday we sat in the men's aisle, second seat on the left. I would read over and over again *Gloria in Excelsis Deo*, a bold statement, perfectly executed in ornate plaster work and gold writing over a most beautiful crucifixion scene in the sanctuary. This scene captured light, balance, colour and strength, the expert draughtsmanship personalising the characters, the narrative forever playing in my head.

On Sunday evenings, it was another visit to the church for Benediction. I sang in the choir, so my view this time was from the lofty gallery at the back of the church. It was the crucifixion scene again. But this time full on and, above it, a low relief, the Lamb of God with six little angels arranged over his head. Six grand pillars, two very large statues of Mother and Child and of Jesus perched in impossibly high niches in the walls. The high altar with two serene angels facing one another, ornate tabernacle door and tall candlesticks placed and spaced with precision. The side altars, under jewelled, stained-glass windows had hand-painted panels with rows of angels and all surfaces throughout the church from doors to walls and window edges were painted with repetitive motifs. The fine-crafted monstrance, the ornate vestments on the priest, the obedient altar boys and the smell of incense never failed to impress me. This sacred space was set apart and separated from the remainder of the church by beautiful altar rails – a subtle boundary but one that commanded the greatest respect.

From this gallery I could enjoy the ornate work of the ceiling like a heavenly sky and the perfect circular plaster centrepiece from which the sanctuary lamp hung by a long chain. This church was special, built in 1857 by the people of Doon parish a few short years after the famine and exactly 100 years before my birth.

Of course, I also noticed the edge that at times permeated the church. While I was still a very young child, the parish missions felt like hours of criticism and disapproval, lightened every now and again by an enthusiastic singing priest. The long evenings with the Canon (the parish priest) calling out the names of the parishioners and the amounts of money they paid into the collection was as near to an evening with Scrooge as one could get! November visits to the local graveyard, which always seemed to be on the darkest of evenings, tested every ounce of my bravery. The poor souls had a bad name, and it felt like there were thousands of them lying in wait just under the sod.

All these visual experiences, which were both ornate and at times dramatic, informed and shaped my thinking. I was feeling even without understanding the richness of symbols. I 'bought' into the message instantly and it never disappointed me.

I was bereft when this church was torn down to its foundations in the early 1970s and nothing prepared me for that great loss and what was for me a very poor replacement. This site of meaning for me was as symbolic in its removal as in its erection. I felt the foundations for my values had been robbed from me and also that the enormous contribution by the people of my parish who must have still been haunted by the Famine when they sacrificed and donated what little they had – including their wedding rings – for this building, was not even considered. My final bittersweet memory of our parish church was the taste of honey – sweet nectar of the gods – after bees had made their home over the entrance door. Industrious generations of bees had spent years saving honey which fell down in golden clumps when it was dislodged by the workers at the start of the demolition. I remember eating it with pieces of wax still in it and, years later, as an art student, I was painfully reminded of this when I first saw Lucas Cranach the Elder's painting, *Cupid complaining to Venus*.

I am second eldest of a family of 10. My older sister, Mary, and I often discuss our childhood. We were spiritual and creative sponges. We were open-hearted and open-minded, far from dismissive, judgemental or half-hearted. As a visual child, 'once upon a time' parables and stories from the New Testament moved me very quickly from reality to fantasy, from awareness of the present to the possibilities of other realities. Listening and surrendering to known and unknown, to seen and unseen. From those biblical stories and images, I built up my childlike notion of welcome in God's house, the compassion and patience he had for little children, and of inclusion and respect. At times, this was in stark contrast with some adults in my life where, with the swish of a veil, I met sarcasm and impatience, where compassion and humanity were lost treasures not for the sharing.

The scene of the Last Judgement (Matthew 25:31–36) seemed simple to me. What else would we do with the sick and the hungry? Why would we not welcome strangers and have compassion for prisoners? My relief when Abraham was rescued in the eleventh hour from having to prove his obedience to God by sacrificing his son Isaac (Genesis 22) had me on edge. To me it never seemed a sensible or even a sane request. I did not understand symbolism or metaphorical concepts then but I was able to suspend my doubts when they were too literal and challenging for me. However, the impact of these first images had made their impression: stained-glass, exquisite motifs and saintly figures in soft pastel colours, pale yellow halos that blurred into blue cloudless skies, serene, safe and special. They all encouraged me to look inwards and had stolen my heart.

Christmas and good tidings thrilled me. My intellectual life depended on religious stories as well as fairy tales. Miracles like the wedding feast at Cana (John 2:1–12) and the parable of the talents – hidden or used (Matthew 25:14–30) – were major contributing factors to my socialisation. They helped me to form my ideas of what life was about and its purpose, and gave me something on which to model myself. The fact that each of my nine siblings is faithfully called after an angel or a saint added another layer of stories. Some were called after a martyr – even more powerful again when viewed in images.

The crucifixion and the horror of betrayal and death traumatised me. Following the images of the 14 Stations of the Cross where I was expected to dwell on suffering and sacrifice at times had me reeling. Easter Sunday mornings after the sad, dark days of the Passion, after the solemn silence of Good Friday which we observed at home from noon until three in the afternoon (at grandmother's insistence), while Jesus died on the cross for us and the long Lenten fast from any sweet treats had me well and truly ready to embrace the resurrection, to believe in the possibility of light and hope returning to life.

The feast of Corpus Christi was pageant-like through our main street, with flower petals strewn by all those little girls who were still able to fit into First Communion dresses. My memory is of the array of altars on each window or doorway on our main street. Lilac always seemed to bloom, and religious statues and white starched altar cloths from each household made their way out into the light to be admired and to celebrate the Host in our beautiful monstrance being carried through the street. The blue cloaks of the Children of Mary, who were indeed very mature women, added a great splash of colour and I remember many of them, on dying during the years that followed, were 'laid out' in that same blue and then buried with those very large medals on their chests.

My teenage years presented everything as a trial, in both church and school. Everything about being a teenager was viewed as unacceptable. Yet the poorest example and behaviour I witnessed was from the very people blessed with vocations, and my disillusionment was profound. My task then was to readjust to the diluted and often distorted message of the gospel. But it would be unfair not to acknowledge some excellent teachers who always seemed to restore my faith and helped me bypass my disillusionment.

Painting and exploring creativity was an inner necessity for me and, luckily, one that was recognised and facilitated by my family. Art making as a non-verbal language seemed to communicate perfectly my thoughts and feelings. The richness of symbols and the fascination of storytelling were the best vehicles with which to do this. Creativity was my way of expressing myself, solving problems and shaping my world. I believe that is why I connected so much to the imagery in my parish church, to the meticulous craftsmanship and the makers' motivation, and to the symbolism that was so intuitive and meditative.

When I was 17 years old, as a member of the Legion of Mary I went on *Peregrinatio Pro Christo* (commonly known as PPC) to

n Scotland. I was ill-prepared, unsafe as it happened,
I was rescued by my hosts, Joe and Cathy Harkins.
...eir interpretation of what it meant to be a Catholic felt to me
deeper, richer and wiser. Again, this helped me to bypass my
disillusionment. I spent the following summer in London with
my friend Theo, before I enrolled in Art College. It was a natural
thing for us to visit galleries and museums because we both
loved art. But that summer was also a time when I found myself
coming face to face with religious paintings and it was the
beginning of my wistfulness over what was lost.

I remember my first time seeing Tinterotto's *Jesus washing the
feet of his disciples*, an almost domestic scene, mainly dark with
the figure of Jesus glowing with a subtle halo. I then remembered a particular Holy Thursday when local men from Doon
had been chosen to be the 12 apostles while our parish priest
washed their feet at the altar. It was indeed theatrical.

I saw one beautiful altar piece after another hanging in these
galleries and museums, removed from their intended sites. I
certainly lost count of how many heads of John the Baptist and
Salome I saw. I also saw crucifixion scenes that were at times
painted by artists with such an intensity that they were often
more savage than compassionate. Although I never forgot
Bassano's image of *The Way to Calvary*, with Veronica and those
beautifully painted plaits in her hair, holding a cloth while
Jesus seemed detached and separate from the crowd. For me,
this captured a moment of true compassion. In stark contrast
were devotional panels such as Fra Lippo Lippi's *Annunciation*
packed with the symbolic language of lilies and the walled
garden all alluding to purity and virginity. Each painting of a
saint carried further symbols (usually the instruments of their
death). I knew that these images were impacting on me but I
was unable to respond in any way that was comfortable for me.

Art connects; it reminds and it mirrors and, in the main, religious works encourage compassion. However, when viewed
in a museum or art gallery, we have to hold back from our religious responses. We can hardly kneel and pray because this
might interrupt the other gallery visitors. So we learn to pay a
different kind of homage, to measure our response and, instead,
we admire the skills and techniques. But I now understand that

these images still have the power to reach us at many extraordinary levels and to feed and fulfil needs and desires that we cannot put into words.

My first viewing of El Greco's *Saint Francis Receiving the Stigmata* in the National Gallery in Dublin was like a jolt. This painting from the sixteenth century had a very modern feel to it, capturing a moment and conveying a feeling through colour and distorted shapes, and it took a small step away from reality. El Greco was considered an outsider artist. He was independent in his methods and I believe this is what attracted me to the work; the feeling and mood in his work brought me back to my childhood church with its natural drama captured in earthy pigments.

My grandmother was very proud of her relative Gabriel Hayes and her 18-year project of carving life-size stations of the cross for Galway cathedral. I understand that this connection facilitated a respect for art in my home and my desire to go to Art College. While at college in Limerick, I met Benedict Tutty, a Benedictine monk from Glenstal Abbey. His facility to explore religious themes in wood and clay, in metal and paint, and his encouragement for me to look further than the surface of my work was the beginning of a more conscious looking.

Benedict introduced me to the work of Patrick Pye and I was fascinated by his primitive style of image-making and how he repeated themes such as the *Agony in the Garden* so often as if it was an event he needed to revisit and connect with on a regular basis. Benedict was a contemporary artist who brought his personal engagement with his faith to his work which was, for me, full of spirit. He encouraged that very personal outing of faith and art.

In 1990, I became artist in residence in St Joseph's Psychiatric Hospital in Limerick. I related to the work and the people living out their lives there with ease. On the grounds of the hospital was a small church dedicated to St Dymphna, the patron saint of mental illness. It was still in use at that time and I occasionally attended Mass there, which was a mixture of sounds and movements and participation unlike anything I had experienced before.

The participants in my art sessions were all long-term residents, some having spent in excess of 40 years in the hospital. I realised that the 30 people engaging in creative activities weekly, very quickly attached great meaning to their paintings and drawings. The image was the messenger and a non-judgemental and accepting witness was all that was required. One very individualistic and creative man called John Bourke painted with me every day for 14 years. Before his death, he was recognised and celebrated as an outsider artist. John was fuelled again by this inner necessity to create. He explored a variety of themes in his work: birds, flowers and wildlife. He also painted religious themes: angels, saints, the Sacred Heart and the Crown of Thorns were often repeated. Also in his work he regularly revisited the church of St Peter and St Paul in Kilmallock, County Limerick. John was admitted to St Joseph's Hospital in 1958 when he 17 years of age, yet his memory and attention to details of steeple, rose windows, buttresses and the surrounding landscape of his childhood church was breathtaking. Each day at noon John said the Angelus. He stopped painting, stood up, joined his hands and, smiling, he prayed aloud and was absorbed. He reminded me of the painting *The Angelus* by Millet, taking a moment of respite and connection.

One touching piece by John was of St Francis surrounded by animals and birds, the saint's qualities forever captured in a gentle and open pose. John bought into his early childhood spirituality and creativity and nothing in all his years of misunderstanding and institutional care ever stole it from him. He cultivated the healthy part of himself, paid attention to it and was rescued by it.

I decided to train as an art therapist because it made perfect sense to me to marry my own art making and the richness and wisdom of symbolism with this new career. Art connects and is often a way in which to tell the stories of our lives and to access unexpressed feelings. While I arrived in St Joseph's Hospital at a time when much was being addressed regarding institutionalisation, it is fair to say that I met remnants and fragments of once whole people. If ever the need for patience and respect, inclusion and compassion were called for, it was here. Compassionate rage propelled me and I tried to use the language of art to break down the lonely and silent separation between the patients and myself. We have come a long way in our understanding and treatment of mental health challenges. Yet the terror experienced by anyone in a psychotic episode still has to feel like a tsunami. The territory that has to be managed by somebody in deep depression is frightening and lonely. I could just imagine how difficult it would have been to convince anyone of recovery in those early days. Choices were few. People become wild with frustration, or silent and withdrawn with apathy. Neither satisfied those who had the power to set the person free.

Praying and begging God for mercy would need to be done in a very orderly and measured fashion so as not to arouse any further suspicion regarding one's mental state. Religiosity was suspect. Minds that at one time may have been adrift were forever kept in hospital. Confidence in our thoughts and beliefs is often taken for granted, but when it is shaken and challenged it is very difficult to know where to turn. This doubt can then become double-edged and the greatest obstacle to spiritual and mental well-being, because how do we know and how do we trust what are sometimes extraordinary and supernatural experiences? There was a very different view on 'seen and unseen' within those walls and who gets to be the saint and who gets to be the madman was a loaded question.

When on holidays I visit churches. The Catholic past in me meets the Catholic present and I am reminded of what was lost in Doon church, where the richness of the symbols was erased forever. I light candles which keep vigil for me for hours after I leave and I am in awe at how these buildings have survived and are protected and cared for, and how fragments and time-worn artefacts are treasured and preserved. It does not matter that I do not understand nor am I able to read the many symbols in these buildings. I know they are working on other levels to feed and nourish me.

When I first walked under Michelangelo's ceiling in the Sistine Chapel in the Vatican, I remember from my art history that he was a very unwilling artist and this great work, started in 1508, was completed through great urging from Pope Julius II. Yet somewhere along the way Michelangelo must have been inspired and guided by those stories from Genesis as he painted backwards from the Flood to the Creation.

I am consoled and frustrated by the labyrinth in Chartres Cathedral in France, and I am reminded that life is anything but straightforward. The flying buttresses in Notre Dame Cathedral in Paris always remind me of friends lending support. St Mary's basilica in Krakow – frantic on the inside with gold decoration and beautifully stained-glass windows – is a treasure trove of monuments to a spiritual life. Yet the short train journey from this Catholic church to the 'Gates of Hell' in Auschwitz tells me that sanity and insanity live very close together and that we all need to pay attention to our moral compass and regularly reset it to compassion.

I no longer practice my faith outwardly. I feel unable to do so because of some of the choices I have made in my life. But it is a strange coincidence that I now paint in a studio on the top floor of the former Franciscan Friary in Limerick city,[1] which inspired me to write the poem at the end of this essay. The church, now deconsecrated, still holds mystery and sacredness for me. I love that the communication and conversation still runs like a prayer in my head regardless of all that is lost. That the artwork still draws my eyes heavenwards, as was intended. Fragments excite me, as they give me good reason to continue my search. Faded or broken, in a way these shards point to a complete beauty elsewhere, which I imagine is greater and grander. That is where I imagine my belief is stuck, content for now with fragments, knowing all will fall into a perfect order in time.

Sacred Fragments
I want to paint fragments
Faded treasures
Once loved objects
Beauty, washed out almost scrubbed clean
Torn, precious gold leaf.

No more light filled moments.
Let me dwell on loss, on change
On once true truths, now dusty with neglect.

---

1. The inspiration for the painting on the cover of this book.

Mould threatened colours
Fragments rich and true
No longer making a whole, only in my mind.

Beauty in decay
Where magic has been taken away
No more hosts nor monstrances
Nor bells ringing time.
(*Gerry Carew*, June 2011)

My hope in Catholicism

Dermot Mannion

'Jesus I have faith, please help what little faith I have' (Mark 9:14–29). This is one of my favourite quotes, one which sums up how fragile our faith can be.

These are uncertain times for Christians. History shows that the church has always suffered attacks and there have been many horrific self-inflicted wounds along the way. Today, a new form of political correctness has emerged which has declared 'open season' on Christian values, while other belief systems are being protected from scrutiny or analysis. However, our Christian faith persists because it is based on hope.

Hope is a fundamental part of the human condition. To quote a famous line from the great movie *The Shawshank Redemption*: 'Hope is a good thing, maybe the best of things and good things never die.'

A good example of the pursuit of hope is Spirit FM (www.spiritradio.ie). This is the first ever multi-denominational national Christian radio station in Ireland. Spirit plays a lively mix of popular music together with interview and phone-in programmes; all designed to deliver a positive message of hope, especially to young people in an otherwise very challenging world. Spirit FM is a not-for-profit station, which is funded almost entirely by charitable donations. Already the station is making a real difference in Ireland. It receives a constant stream of wonderful messages from listeners who have been uplifted by something they heard on air. It is a venture that is most worthy of support.

Many of our ancestors in Ireland grew up with this same sense of hope and faith which has been passed down through the generations. Three of my grandparents were very much part of this great tradition. However, my maternal grandmother's story was different and it bears repeating.

Her name was Jesse Lowe and she was born into a Presbyterian family in Scotland and was sent to Ireland to work for the 'landed gentry' on a large estate in Sligo. On one level, her story has a romantic aspect to it. She worked in a castle and fell in love and married the driver, my grandfather Ned.

However, on another level Jesse suffered many hardships along the way, especially for her faith, but she never lost hope. She went on to have seven daughters and provided an outstanding example of simple faith, hard work and good humour to all her grandchildren, including me. Jesse was an early advocate for ecumenism in the manner in which she treated people of all faiths and none just the same.

I have great memories of time spent in her house on summer holidays, getting washed and scrubbed on Saturday night, ready to wear our Sunday best for Mass the next morning. Sunday Mass was a very big deal in Jesse's life, which has left a very big impression on me.

Another of my early memories of Mass is walking the few miles from Sligo to the Holy Well at Tobarnalt, which I regularly did as a child with my parents. Hidden away among the trees and close to the lake, this was the perfect place of seclusion to celebrate the Mass in Penal times. What risk to life and limb the faithful of previous generations took in coming to worship in this place. They were a people of faith, hope and courage who never gave up despite their challenges.

I have been very humbled to meet people from other countries around the world, whose faces light up at the very mention of Ireland. The reason being that they received a good education from Irish missionaries which lifted them out of poverty and brought such hope into their lives. It is sad to see the current move to drive the religious orders out of Irish education; as a nation, we will be the poorer for their passing.

Many seeds of the Irish missionary movement were sown at Mass rocks such as Tobarnalt which continue to be symbols of hope even today. Each July on Garland Sunday, the lives and sufferings of those who worshipped at Tobarnalt are celebrated, starting with a sunrise Mass.

My most recent attendance at this Mass was memorable. On this particular July morning, instead of the expected good weather, a storm had been blowing all night with strong winds and heavy rain. However, by the time Mass began at 6 a.m., there was a sudden calm and the sun even managed to break through the clouds. It was a serene moment in a beautiful setting and here again we could not fail to come away uplifted and full of hope.

It is such a shame we have become so complacent and blasé about attendance at Mass these days. In previous generations, the faithful understood the full significance of the Mass and the 'Real Presence', with Jesus being 'beaten, broken and crushed'[1] just as wheat is in the making of the Host.

Another of my earliest memories as a boy is being dragged along by my parents to assist the priest at Benediction in the local church. I just loved the smell of the burning incense which has stayed with me to this day. For the longest time, Benediction and Adoration seemed to have gone into decline. However, with the encouragement of Pope John Paul the Great and Pope Benedict XVI there are new shoots of hope and signs of a resurgence. This is especially evident since the conclusion of the very successful Eucharistic Congress in Dublin 2012.

Recently, a bishop from the Far East visited the adoration chapel at the Cathedral of the Immaculate Conception in Sligo, which has now been in operation for 22 years. He was sufficiently impressed to go back to his own parish and kick start Eucharistic Adoration with the hope that momentum will build and the parishioners will see the benefit.

We all need much more time and space in which to think, away from the noise and hustle and bustle of the day to day world. In the Internet age of instant reaction and communication it is hard, but nonetheless most worthwhile, to find the patience necessary to just sit in silence and to shut the rest of the world out: '... trials produce patience, from patience comes merit, merit is the source of hope and hope does not disappoint us' (Romans 5:3–5).

Devotion to Mother Mary was another big feature of my youth and is yet another source of great hope in the lives of people today. I was reminded of this recently when I came across a new novena dedicated to Our Lady Undoer of Knots (www.ourladyundoerofknots.com). This devotion started with

---

1   Lucia, Vincent Martin, *Come to Me in the Blessed Eucharist* (Missionaries of the Blessed Sacrament, 1993).

a painting by a German artist which has been venerated in the Church of St Peter in Augsburg, Germany since the year 1700.

It is an extraordinary painting. Above the head of Our Lady is the Holy Spirit – guiding her hand. Meanwhile an angel is shown handing a very tangled piece of rope to Mother Mary, who in turn gently untangles it and passes it back. I find the image in this picture striking and so powerful. It conveys formidable strength, yet there is also great tenderness.

This powerful message was strongly reinforced when I was asked to speak at a special faith formation week in a parish in Dublin. I had never spoken publicly on faith matters before and found the whole experience very intimidating. However, as soon as I showed the image of Mary Undoer of Knots, she completely stole the show. Copies of the novena booklet went like hotcakes and I am told they have been passed around the world to family and friends. The tangled 'rope' truly begets hope in the hands of Our Lady.

I also have vivid memories of the Rosary from my youth, yet another vehicle of hope in our lives. May is the month of Our Lady and every year a special altar was prepared in our house, usually decorated with primroses from the garden. Every night without fail for the whole month, my parents would get all eight children down on our knees to pray the Rosary. A ritual not always enjoyed by us as children but one that has remained with me into adult life.

Padre Pio called the Rosary beads his weapon in the war of good against evil. In recent years, I have become active as a volunteer with www.worldpriest.com, a website run by lay people which is dedicated to providing resources to support priests worldwide. Worldpriest promotes the annual Rosary Relay for priests which now covers the whole world, with 60 countries praying the Rosary in an unbroken chain across the full 24 hours of a single day. Each year the participation by parishes and prayer groups is showing enormous growth, which again represents a great beacon of hope for the future.

The following story illustrates the power of the Rosary:

An old man and a young student shared a carriage on a train in France. The student noticed that the old man was quietly praying the Rosary, feeding the beads through his fingers. He plucked up the courage to speak to the old man: 'Sir, why do you concern yourself with all that old stuff, this is the new age of science?' The old man smiled in amusement and gently asked, 'What is this new age of science?' The student continued, 'Sir, give me your address and I will send you some material on this.'

Finally, the old man shuffled in his pocket for a pen and wrote shakily on a piece of paper and handed it to the student. The paper read 'Louis Pasteur, Scientist.' After a lifetime of dedication to science, if the Rosary is good enough for Louis Pasteur, it is good enough for me!

Looking to the future, undoubtedly there will be many challenges to be faced in our lives. However, the great richness of our Christian and Catholic heritage will help us to cling to 'what little faith we have' and face the future full of hope.

> Hope is the thing with feathers
> That perches in the soul,
> And sings the tune without the words,
> And never stops at all,
>
> And sweetest in the gale is heard;
> And sore must be the storm
> That could abash the little bird
> That kept so many warm.
>
> I've heard it in the chillest land,
> And on the strangest sea;
> Yet, never, in extremity,
> It asked a crumb of me.
> (Emily Dickinson)

Hope is indeed 'a good thing, maybe the best of things and good things will never die'.

The love of Christ is a service, not a sentiment

Finola Kennedy

From the start, my Catholicism has been about people – my parents, my sisters, my teachers, my friends. It has been about the person of Christ, the person who was so attractive that people left their parents, their teachers and their friends to be with him. And it has been about Mary, the Mother of Christ, and St Joseph.

Catholicism for me is the life of Christ. Before his birth, Mary was asked if she would consent to be his mother. She agreed. A perplexed Joseph accepted the situation. Jesus was born in a stable in Bethlehem. He learned to be a man from Joseph. But he later went about his 'Father's business' in the Temple and left Joseph and Mary bereft. He plied his trade as a carpenter. Then for three years he gathered apostles and disciples and explained to them all that he knew. At the Last Supper and Calvary, he gave us his body and blood in the Eucharist. Three days later he rose from the dead, appearing first to Mary Magdalene.

Since his resurrection, the life of Christ continues through the church or Mystical Body. The central teaching of the Catholic Church is that together we form the One Body of Christ. Mary, who brought Christ into the world in the flesh, was given to us by Christ from the cross to continue the work of bringing him into the world. Christ asks that he be seen and served in *every* human person. This is a radical view of social relations which goes beyond mere equality. For the Christian, Christ *is* every man, woman and child. We are called to respect, serve and love our fellow human being as Christ himself.

The centrality of Christ was emphasised one day when I went to confession in Clarendon Street Church in Dublin. I expressed dismay at a comment made by the Pope. To my astonishment, and counter to my expectation, the elderly confessor said to me, 'No man, not even the Pope, should be allowed to block your view of Jesus Christ.'

I have a memory of an episode when I was very young – I can't remember if I had started school at the time – but I often thought about it later as an early lesson in true religion. My mother had promised to take me to visit Santa Claus in Pim's store in George's Street, Dublin. It was a dark, cold winter day; I was wearing a blue coat and a pair of grey fur gloves, perhaps squirrel.

At the entrance to Pim's, we met a girl about my own age. She had been crying and was dirty. Looking back I think she was probably a traveller child. My mother stopped to talk to her. Worse still, she invited her to come to Santa Claus with us. At the end we both got presents from Santa. Then we parted. I was seething with resentment. I did not want to share my mother with that grubby stranger.

Today if I hurry past a huddled mass of humanity on a footpath or in an alcove, a picture of my mother's spontaneous reaching out to that child may come into my mind. It is a challenging thing to call oneself a Christian – the requirements are challenging. At last count I had seven coats.

My mother remained a committed Catholic to the day she died when I was 15, although she embodied elements of the feminist anti-clericalism battle long before I was born. From a modest Kerry background she made her way, via a grind school and a job in the Post Office, to medical studies in Trinity College Dublin. When I was born, my mother was 38 and my father was 55. I had two older sisters, Peggy and Deirdre, who were respectively eight and six years older than me. I was the spoilt youngest from the word 'Go'.

I attended kindergarten and junior school at Loreto Beaufort, Rathfarnham. Many of the nuns in Beaufort had the names of male saints including Sr John Bosco who taught catechism. We learned answers to questions, such as, 'Who made the world?' We memorised prayers including the Confiteor and the Apostles' Creed which I did not understand but could repeat rapidly.

At the time it seemed that there was an answer for every question. Sometimes I wasn't entirely satisfied, as when I asked the nun, 'Who made God?' I'm not sure if she thought I was being cheeky but she replied gently and confidently that, when I had studied more and finished the course, I would have learned the answer.

Not satisfied, I asked my father. He told me that sometimes we can't understand everything. Then he added that everything I needed was in the 'Our Father'. It took me years to get an inkling of what he meant. At the time I was fascinated by words. What were 'trespasses'? I had seen signs which said 'Trespassers will be prosecuted', but I had not linked the two words.

Preparation for First Confession included practice visits to the chapel in Loreto Abbey, the boarding school across the road from Beaufort. The actual event went off smoothly. At the time 'disobedience' was my favourite sin. I remember my First Communion day vividly. While the rest of my class received their First Communion in the Abbey chapel, I received my First Communion in the chapel of the Sisters of Charity at Mount St Anne's in Milltown where my late aunt, Sr Padua Flanagan, had been a nun. Years later I learned that she had written the first life of Mother Mary Aikenhead, the founder of the Sisters of Charity. Following Mass we were given breakfast by the nuns and then one of the nuns took me to inspect the hens and to collect eggs.

Growing up on the remains of a farm in Walkinstown, we belonged to the Crumlin parish where Canon Hickey was parish priest. He lived in a big house beside the church. He had a housekeeper who wore a uniform. He kept greyhounds. The church had a penny door at the back and a sixpenny door at the side. I usually went to the nine o'clock Mass with my father on Sundays.

On weekdays my mother and I often went to the 7.30 a.m. Mass at Drimnagh Castle where the Christian Brothers had a school. The early morning walks across to Drimnagh Castle were the start of a habit of daily Mass which I continued imperfectly throughout my life. To an extent daily Mass has become a routine but I think that over the years I've begun to get a small insight into the reality. Being present at Mass can be complicated by different priests with different styles. More and more I tend to close my eyes and try to be there. That is I try to cast my mind back to the Last Supper and Calvary. I find Mary is a big help because she was freely there and she stood upright at the Cross. How did she cope?

Just before finishing junior school, I was confirmed by Archbishop John Charles McQuaid in Rathfarnham Church. For some reason we were worried that we might be unable to answer a catechism question posed by the Archbishop and thus 'fail' or not be permitted to receive the sacrament. In the event he passed over me, so I was not put to the test.

The family Rosary was a feature of my life as a child. Each decade was called a 'mystery'. I had absolutely no idea what some of the words meant. What was 'the fruit of thy womb?' It would be a while before I understood the word 'womb'. It was much longer before I learned Newman's great insight that the Rosary makes the Creed into a prayer.

In the senior school I moved to Our Lady's School in Terenure. There my mind was opened by a truly remarkable group of teachers including a number of English nuns and a gifted teacher of Irish and French, Maureen Gavan-Duffy. I thrived at Our Lady's. Studying became a pleasure. I got good reports, although my parents never said much about them. When I started some serious study at weekends for the Leaving Certificate my father would often drop in with chocolate biscuits and urge me to go off and play tennis.

A big cloud was the start of my mother's illness when I was 13. She died from breast cancer two years later. Some months before my mother died, I remember sitting on her bed at home and we talked about death. She told me that she had been close to death a few weeks earlier and that she had not been afraid. She also said that as a doctor she had been at many bedsides when people died and that in the main death was peaceful. I sat beside my eldest sister, Peggy, 24 years later, as she too died from breast cancer at a young age. She was fully conscious until about two hours before she died a death which was peace itself. Peggy's hallmark was courage.

The school motto in Our Lady's was *Maria Vitae Porta* (Mary Gate of Life). I was the first Head Girl in Our Lady's and rather than a badge with 'Head Girl' I was given a medal of Mary with a crown of 12 stars. Sometimes when I see an EU blue flag with the 12 gold stars, I wonder how many people realise the origin of the flag.

A branch of the Pioneer Total Abstinence Association was formed in school. We could not become full pioneers until the age of 16 but the question of becoming a probationer arose before my mother died. The nuns had mixed views on the Pioneers. I asked my parents. My mother said that she did not think I would become an alcoholic and that a glass of sherry wasn't a bad thing.

My father, who had gone through a stage of heavy drinking when he returned from the Great War as a young man, became a Pioneer just before he married. He said to me, 'You know it's a funny thing but in my drinking days when I saw someone with a Pioneer badge I felt a twinge of envy.' He was probably the least envious person I ever met in my life and his remark made me think. So I signed up. Now, decades later, I am on the whole glad. Who knows but my mother could have been wrong.

Frank Duff, the founder of the Legion of Mary, was a friend of my parents. My father was a contemporary of his and I think they may have first met in the Society of St Vincent de Paul. My parents asked him to be my godfather, a role which he accepted. Sometimes my father and I would visit him and he would always ask me about myself – about school and tennis. Occasionally he visited our home.

When I left school I spent a year at university in Fribourg, Switzerland before attending UCD (University College Dublin). When I went to Fribourg I knew nothing about the Legion of Mary except that they ran hostels for homeless people, and my father used to buy cigarettes, mostly for the women, I think. It came as a big surprise to me that one of the first people I met in Fribourg was Rosemarie Savignon from Gibraltar. When she heard that I was from Dublin she became quite excited and told me that she had been in the Legion of Mary in Gibraltar. She had discovered that there was a branch of the Legion in the university. She invited me to come with her to a meeting.

My Catholicism was about to take a big step. I began to learn the Legion system. It involved a weekly meeting and a commitment to around two hours of voluntary work of service each week. One also prayed the *Magnificat* daily. Legionary service is rooted in a devotional system with the Eucharist at its core.

My first Legion work was taking blind children for walks and accompanying an elderly lady who lived up several flights of steps, on visits to her doctor. A wonderful Dominican priest attended our meetings without fail and I learned that the church really works when lay people and the priest work together.

On my return to Dublin I was in a student *praesidium* for a number of years, visiting the skin and cancer wards in the old Hume Street hospital. Later I was in the Legion in Cambridge where there was a flourishing group. The president, Pat Mullen, had been Head Boy in Stonyhurst. I remember getting a lift to the Legion meeting on the back of his motorbike.

When my first child was born I resigned from active membership in the Legion. The moment of my first son's birth was an epiphany. When I saw that tiny person who seemed deep in thought, I believed in a Creator. Years later I understood the words of the Psalmist:

> You created my inmost self,
> Knit me together in my mother's womb
> For so many marvels I thank you;
> A wonder am I, and all your works are wonders.

I did not rejoin the Legion for over 20 years. For around 15 of those years I attended a once monthly Patrician Group organised by the Legion. The object of the Patricians is to develop knowledge of Catholicism. The group which I attended and which continues to thrive was originally started for staff at UCD where I worked as a lecturer in economics.

Kieran and I have been blessed with our children – who are no longer 'children' – and our granddaughter. As Kieran's health has failed, the children have been magnificent. So now I am learning Christ's way from my children just as I first learned it from my parents all those years ago.

Editors

JOHN LITTLETON, a priest of the Diocese of Cashel and Emly, is Director of The Priory Institute, Tallaght, Dublin. Among his recent books are *Journeying through the Year of Matthew* (2010) and *The Fulfilment of God's Saving Promise* (2012). With Eamon Maher, he co-edited *What Being Catholic Means to Me* (2009) and *The Dublin/Murphy Report: A Watershed for Irish Catholicism?* (2010). He is a weekly columnist with *The Catholic Times*.

EAMON MAHER is Director of the National Centre for Franco–Irish Studies at the Institute of Technology, Tallaght. Editor of the highly successful *Reimagining Ireland* book series with Peter Lang Oxford, his recent books include *'The Church and its Spire': John McGahern and the Catholic Question* (2010) and (with Catherine Maignant) *Franco–Irish Connections in Space and Time: Peregrinations and Ruminations* (2012). He is currently co-editing with Eugene O'Brien a book of essays entitled *From Prosperity to Austerity: A Socio–Cultural Critique of the Celtic Tiger and its Aftermath*.

Contributors

MARTIN BYRNE is a Christian Brother who teaches in a variety of agencies in Dublin's inner city. For the past 14 years, with the people of the North Wall, he has been involved in a process of urban, contextual theology.

GERRY CAREW is an artist and an art therapist. She works in an acute psychiatric hospital setting. Her art is inspired by several themes including landscape, portraiture and religion. As well as painting locally, she has painted in Canada, France and Italy.

PATRICK CLAFFEY is a member of the Society of the Divine Word. He worked as a missionary in Togo (1977–1986) and the Republic of Benin (1997–2002). Following postgraduate studies at the School of Oriental and African Studies, University of London, he was head of the Department of Mission Theology and Culture at the Milltown Institute in Dublin. He is currently a curate in Dublin and lectures in the study of religions at University College Cork, Trinity College Dublin and All Hallows College Dublin. He has published several books and articles and is currently working on an edited volume *Broken Faith: Why Hope Matters* with Joe Egan and Marie Keenan due for publication later this year.

RICHARD CLARKE is the Church of Ireland Bishop of Meath and Kildare. Prior to his appointment there in 1996, he served in the ordained ministry in Northern Ireland, in Dublin and in Cork, latterly as Dean of Cork. He is the author of two books, *And Is it True?* (2000) and *A Whisper of God* (2006), in addition to a number of articles (primarily in the areas of social theology, ecumenism and church history). He is currently the chair of the Church of Ireland's Commission for Christian Unity and Dialogue.

PETER COSTELLO is an author, critic and editor based in Dublin, who has written, edited or contributed to some 38 books, among them *The Heart Grown Brutal*, about the literature of the Irish revolution, *James Joyce: The Years of Growth*, and *John Stanislaus Joyce*, a biography written with John Wyse Jackson. He is the Honorary Librarian of the Central Catholic Library, Books Editor of *The Irish Catholic* and Chairman of the Friends of the Library of Trinity College Dublin. His most recent publication is an edition of G.K. Chesterton's *Christendom in Dublin*.

BERNADETTE FLANAGAN is Director of Research at All Hallows College, Dublin City University. She has recently co-edited *Spiritual Capital: Spirituality in Practice in Christian Perspective*, with Michael O'Sullivan SJ (2012). She is a member of the International Society for the Study of Christian Spirituality (SSCS), the Mystical Theology Network and the British Association for the Study of Spirituality

ANGELA HANLEY is a theology graduate and is currently engaged in postgraduate studies in moral theology. She is the author of *Justified by Faith: An Irish Missionary Experience in Malawi* (2002) and co-editor of *Quench Not the Spirit, Theology and Prophecy for the Church in the Modern World* (2005). She is married to Gearóid O'Brien and they have two adult children.

MICHAEL KELLY, a native of County Tyrone, is Editor of *The Irish Catholic* newspaper and a writer and broadcaster on religious and social affairs.

FINOLA KENNEDY is author of the pioneering study, *Cottage to Crèche: Family Change in Ireland* (2001). Her latest book, *Frank Duff: A Life Story* (2011), has been a best-seller.

MARY KENNY is a well-known journalist with, among other broad-sheets, the *Irish Independent* and *The Irish Catholic*. As a founding member of the Irish Women's Liberation Movement, she campaigned actively for the legalisation of contraception. Author of several books, her *Goodbye to Catholic Ireland* (1997, 2000) probably remains the best known.

PATRICIA KIERAN formerly lectured in theology and religious education at Newman College, University of Birmingham and she currently teaches at Mary Immaculate College, University of Limerick. She is co-author of *Children, Catholicism and Religious Education* (2005) and co-editor of *Exploring Theology: Making Sense of the Catholic Tradition* (2007), *Exploring Religious Education: Catholic Religious Education in an Intercultural Europe* (2008). Most recently she co-edited *New Educational Horizons in Contemporary Ireland: Trends and Challenges* (2012).

JOHN LONERGAN is a native of Bansha, County Tipperary. He served in the Irish Prison Service for over 42 years. He was Governor of Mountjoy Prison for over 22 years and Governor of the top security prison at Portlaoise for 4 years. He retired in June 2010 and later that year his autobiography, *The Governor*, was published. His philosophy is that change, personal or otherwise, cannot be enforced on people, and he believes that real and meaningful change only comes about through dialogue, consent and agreement. He is convinced that people change from the inside out. He suggests that the big task for all of us as human beings is to find the humanity in others and then to nurture it. He believes that the more people are in touch with their own humanity the more likely they are to treat others with humanity.

ANGELA MACNAMARA was actively involved in the area of relationships education in schools before becoming a well-known national figure as an advice columnist for the *Sunday Press* from 1963 until 1980. Her published work includes *Will Our Children Build Healthy Relationships?*, *Ready, Steady Grow* and the memoir *Yours Sincerely*. She is now an occasional journalist and speaker.

MAIREAD McGUINNESS, an MEP since 2004, is an agricultural economist and food policy expert. She focuses on the future shape of agriculture and rural development, global development policy, the environment and food safety and security. She was voted MEP of the Year for agriculture in 2011. Prior to becoming an MEP, she was a well-known journalist, broadcaster and commentator.

DERMOT MANNION is currently Deputy Chairman of Royal Brunei Airlines in the Far East. Previously he was Chief Executive of Aer Lingus in Dublin and before that President Group Services of Emirates Airline in Dubai. He is a graduate of Trinity College Dublin and is a fellow of the Institute of Chartered Accountants in Ireland. Mr Mannion is also a non-executive director of Spirit FM, Ireland's first nationwide Christian radio station which is run on a 'not-for-profit' basis.

GAY MITCHELL is an MEP for Dublin, former Lord Mayor of Dublin and Minister for European Affairs. He was a TD for 26 years.

MARIE MURRAY, clinical psychologist, author and broadcaster, has worked as a psychologist for almost 40 years and as an *Irish Times* columnist for eight years. She is a former Director of UCD Student Counselling Services and she is a Member of the Medical Council of Ireland.

NÓIRÍN NÍ RIAIN is a renowned spiritual singer and was awarded the first ever doctorate in theology from Mary Immaculate College, University of Limerick in 2003. She currently lives in Glenstal Abbey where she runs regular workshops on many aspects of theology and chant. An author, she has written several books, the most recent being on her doctoral research entitled *Theosony: Towards a Theology of Listening* (2011).

RÓNÁN MULLEN was elected to represent the National University of Ireland constituency in Seanad Éireann in July 2007. He is an independent senator and was re-elected, topping the poll, in 2011. After studying in University College Galway and spending a year as President of the Students Union there, he held various positions but became well known as a spokesperson for the Dublin diocese between 1996 and 2001. In 2003 he was called to the Bar. He also lectures in law, communications and personal development in the Institute of Technology in Blanchardstown. Rónán is from Ahascragh in County Galway.

WILLIE WALSH is a native of Roscrea, County Tipperary. After his ordination in Rome in 1959 and then some years of studying for a doctorate in canon law, he returned to teach in Saint Flannan's Ennis (County Clare). He was very prominent for a number of years in ACCORD (formerly the Catholic Marriage Advisory Council), before being appointed Coadjutor Bishop and then Bishop of Killaloe in 1994. He retired from that position in 2011.